REAL ESTATE
OFFICE MANAGEMENT
A GUIDE TO SUCCESS

ROBERT L. HERD
CRB, CRS, GRI

CENGAGE
Learning

Australia • Brazil • Japan • Korea • Mexico • Singapore • Spain • United Kingdom • United States

CENGAGE
Learning™

**Real Estate Office
Management:
A Guide to Success**
Robert L. Herd

VP/Executive Publisher:
Dave Shaut

Acquiring Editor: Scott
Person

Developmental Editor:
Sara Froelicher

Sr. Production Editor:
Deanna Quinn

Marketing Manager: Mark
Linton

Manufacturing
Coordinator: Charlene
Taylor

Design Project Manager:
Rik Moore

Internal Designer:
Lou Ann Thesing

Cover Designer:
Rik Moore

Cover Photograph:
PhotoDisc, Inc.

Production House and
Compositor: Carlisle
Publisher Services

Library of Congress Control Number: 2002067000

ISBN-13: 978-0-324-18484-6

ISBN-10: 0-324-18484-0

Cengage Learning
5191 Natorp Boulevard
Mason, OH 45040
USA

Cengage Learning is a leading provider of customized learning
solutions with office locations around the globe, including
Singapore, the United Kingdom, Australia, Mexico, Brazil, and Japan.
Locate your local office at **www.cengage.com/global**

Cengage Learning products are represented in Canada by
Nelson Education, Ltd.

To learn more about Cengage Learning, visit **www.cengage.com**

Purchase any of our products at your local college store or at our
preferred online store **www.CengageBrain.com**

Printed in the United States of America
5 6 7 8 9   16 15 14 13 12

FD272

Contents

Chapter Nine

Chapter Ten

Chapter Eleven

Appendix A

Appendix B

Prologue

What's the difference between a good and a great real estate office manager? In the long run, it all comes down to profits. Why just profits, you ask? Because without profits, you are not in business long and nothing else matters. Businesses exist to perpetuate themselves, providing stable employment for many people and a return on large sums of money put at risk by the owners or investors. But the real difference between a good and a great manager lies in the type of environment that the manager creates for people to create those ever-necessary profits. This is called passion for what you do! The importance of the role of the real estate office manager cannot be understated. He or she is the catalyst that takes a real estate office to unlimited prosperity, allows it to fail, or has it succumb to mediocrity.

My first management position was in a small branch office in California in the early seventies. I assessed the office my first day and found that all but two of the agents were retired from other jobs and had shown virtually no motivation to sell anything. During my second week I called a meeting and set a minimum standard. All of the "retirees" left within the next ten days, and I was free to recruit and train my new sales staff. The broker was furious with me. He roared up to the office in his car and ran into the office. "What are you doing to me?" he yelled. I calmly told him that I had just "repositioned" his office for greater things. My recruiting and training efforts worked out well, and within eight months my office was performing better than the main office that he ran. I had only been in the business a little under two years at the time.

In October of 1974, I opened my own company, a Century 21 franchise. What a heady feeling it was, knowing that I was in complete control of my own destiny! Fortunately I was smart enough to know that my college degree in aircraft maintenance wouldn't help me much in owning and operating a real estate business. Fortunately there was excellent help available, and I soon found myself flying around the country taking the wonderfully designed courses offered by the CRB (Certified Residential Brokerage Manager) Council. These courses are available through the National Association of REALTORS® and include virtually every issue that you can face as a manager, including recruiting, training, retention, business planning, economic trends analysis, effective advertising, and much, much more. They helped immensely, and after the first eighteen months in business my firm had 29 percent of the very active and lucrative north peninsula market.

I worked very hard for the next two years, recruiting as many of the best "go-getters" that I could find, training them, and watching with satisfaction as they grew into some of the best and most productive agents in the entire real estate board. We took every honor that Century 21 had to give over the next several years and quickly became the office of preference in the north peninsula. During my first year of operation, I left over 40 percent of my personal commissions in the company to pay expenses. By the second year, however, I was making an excellent net profit from the company. Could this happen today? Absolutely, under the right circumstances.

I sold my company in the mid-eighties and began working as a branch manager for one of the large residential firms in northern California. I eventually worked for four different companies, including the one that I work for now, managing as many as 145 sales associates at a time. I personally found these positions frustrating and exciting, but most of all rewarding. You may be asking yourself, should I become an owner or manager? Read on, and decide for yourself!

Conversion from Sales to Management: Should You, or Shouldn't You?

A crucial question to ask yourself is: Why do you want to become a manager? Many very successful agents decide to become managers because they are tired of working weekends. Others want the stability of a steady monthly base pay. Still others want the prestige, or feel that being a manager is a "move up." Some just want a new challenge or the opportunity to help influence the lives of other people in a positive way. There are three types of managers. Let's look at each one.

> *A crucial question to ask yourself is: Why do you want to become a manager?*

The Selling Manager

The selling manager is a broker/owner or office manager who is still allowed to maintain his or her own sales and listing activities while conducting his or her management duties. This is a given for the person opening his or her own firm, as budget concerns seldom allow otherwise. Newly formed companies and new branch offices of existing companies seldom have the immediate cash flow or operating budget to pay for a full-time non-selling manager. They will often hire a sales agent as manager and compensate him or her with a higher commission split on his or her personal sales as well as a percentage of the net operating profits, if any. Other types of pay include recruiting bonuses for each agent recruited and medical/dental benefits.

Recruiting

If the manager recruits several good people who quickly become productive, he or she can receive some excellent bonuses. If the manager's personal sales are good, the higher commission split can really make a difference. The problem with this type of compensation is that much of it works in direct opposition to good management principles.

The manager that suddenly finds himself or herself with an increased commission split is inclined to spend that much more time on his or her personal sales instead of conducting the much-needed management functions. Conversely, if the manager spends too much time on management duties and neglects sales function duties, there may eventually be a shortage of money. If you are going to manage under these circumstances you will need to be very careful to balance your time between the two. I found that I could manage up to thirty agents without cutting into my own sales. Beyond that, I began to lose my personal sales time to the necessary management duties. In supervising over forty agents, I needed to cut my personal sales time way back in order to remain an effective manager. This will obviously vary from person to person but it is definitely something that you need to consider when analyzing your decision to become a manager.

The Non-Selling Manager

If you elect to leave sales entirely and take a position as a non-selling manager, there are several important factors that you will need to consider.

Compensation

Since you will be receiving virtually all of your compensation as a result of other people's achievement, you will need to assess what type of operation you are taking over. If it is a well-run branch office for a major firm, with lots of good agents already in place, then the company's existing compensation schedule may already be adequate.

As a new manager, though, you may be asked to take over an ailing branch office or open a new branch office for the company. If this is the case, be sure to negotiate a minimum salary each month, plus any bonuses tied to either gross income and/or net profits, if any, that is commensurate with the extremely challenging job that you have ahead of you. In both of these cases there is little likelihood that you will see anything but the salary for many months after you take over. If you agree to a minimal salary right away, with the promise of bonuses, you will soon become very discouraged by the lack of immediate monetary rewards.

Most companies are very aware of how important your role is in taking on a new or troubled office, and although you can't expect them to throw money at you, they will usually negotiate a higher-than-normal salary to get you through the start-up or transitional period, which is usually about one year. By then the company will usually expect you to have the operation at or near maximum efficiency, although there are exceptions, such as breaking into a lucrative area where one or more highly dominant companies already exist as competition.

As an example, a recruiting bonus of $500 for every new agent, $1,000 for every experienced agent with less than $100,000 in annual earnings, and $2,000 for every agent with earnings in excess of $100,000 recruited is an excellent type of performance-based compensation, which works very well as an incentive to staff a new or troubled branch.

Expectations

One of the most important things to evaluate and talk over with upper management prior to taking on this type of position is their expectations. How much, how soon is the key question.

> - How much profit does management expect and by what date?
> - What are their key indicators of progress? Gross volume sales, gross office income and/or company dollars retained, net profits, and number of listings and/or sales in a given time period are all indicators used to measure progress.

In 1985 I was offered a position as vice president/manager of a new commercial real estate firm. The money was excellent, but when I asked the owner of the company what his expectations were, I knew that he was way off base. I explained

One of the most important things to evaluate and talk over with upper management prior to taking on this type of position is their expectations.

Ask Yourself These Questions of Upper Management:

- Do you like, or at least respect, the owners and/or the upper management of the company?
- Are they ethical?
- Will they require you to do anything as a manager that you will be uncomfortable with?
- Are they strong enough financially to support you in your new role for a reasonable time?
- How committed are they to making your branch office a permanently viable operation?
- What resources are they willing to commit to you for recruiting and training agents and promoting your office to the local community?

to him in detail why it wouldn't work out, but he was adamant, so I declined the position. The firm closed less than eighteen months later.

Look Before You Leap

Some branch offices are just a bad idea that developed out of someone's inflated ego, or at least very poor research. Before you take a position as a manager, look at the demographics. If you don't see a reasonable chance of success for any reason, don't open the office or take the assignment.

The Top-Performer as a Manager

In the seventies and eighties it was very common to see a person come into real estate, do very well, rise to the top in sales, and then decide to open his or her own firm, only to fail miserably! One of the most important things that you can take with you from this book is that there is not any direct correlation between how good a salesperson you are and how good a manager you will be! The very definition of a manager is someone who attains a predetermined goal through the efforts of others.

Although I know many top-performers, including myself, who have opened highly successful real estate companies or become excellent branch managers, many top-performers have big egos that are often a huge stumbling block to being a good manager. By the very nature of being a manager you are

One of the most important things that you can take with you from this book is that there is not any direct correlation between how good a salesperson you are and how good a manager you will be!

receiving all of your rewards, monetary and otherwise, through the efforts of others; that's the very nature of your job. It is paramount that you tuck your ego in your back pocket and quickly learn to get your ego gratification from being an integral part of the cumulative success of others.

Many top-performer managers have an "I'm great, so it's my way or the highway" attitude toward their sales staff. This simply doesn't work well. While there are certainly success traits that are universal and must be passed on to others, success in real estate sales is a very personalized issue that is as different as each individual. Failure to realize this most often spells failure for the manager that can't allow his sales staff the freedom to "use his garden to grow their own flowers."

Your Personality Type and Style

You have personality traits and styles of interacting with others that are completely unique to you. Your personality creates a unique strength if you let it work for you and will cause you much distress if you ignore it.

What do I mean by this? Your major successes in hiring and working on a day-to-day basis with other agents will mostly come from hiring people that are very similar to you in their personalities and the style in which they do business. You will simply be better able to interact with each other one-on-one and as a group. There are exceptions, of course; however, although you will be able to tolerate an agent that is very different from you, too many of them working for you at one time will leave you exhausted at the end of each day and can easily burn you out as a manager.

The two types of management styles are autocratic and democratic. Most good managers use a little of both, remaining autocratic with the major business decisions and allowing group input about some of the day-to-day operating issues. A good example is if you do an analysis of where your advertising dollars are most effectively spent. You don't want input from agents that don't really know anything about the effectiveness of each of the media vehicles that you choose. However, you may ask for group input on how to handle signing up for and running the floor time schedule. Since they, not you, take the calls, they probably have some good ideas about what will work best.

The main point here is that everyone tends to favor one style more than the other, and you need to know this about yourself so that you will surround yourself with as many highly compatible people as possible.

After you have determined your style of interacting with others (that is, how democratic or autocratic you are), the next issue to determine is your personality type. These personality types can run from the highly direct "go for the sale at all costs" type of personality that is only interested in making the sale, with little or no emphasis on the relationship with the customers, to the "only do it if it feels good" type of personality that is so totally into the client relationship that these people hesitate to help lead the client to a decision and lose the sale. Obviously, neither of these personality type extremes are effective in today's real estate sales environment. The too direct type of person scares off most of today's market savvy consumers as they want information, not sales techniques, and the "I'm your friend" type of person simply lets one opportunity after another go by and, worse yet, causes many consumers to lose a home that they would otherwise have been very happy in.

Do a very honest and close assessment of your style of managing and your personality type and think carefully about it as you interview prospective salespeople.

Chapter

2

Managing for Another Company

*A*s mentioned in Chapter One, as a new manager you will probably not inherit a large, well-run office with lots of top producers and a large annual net profit. Virtually all of the large multi-office companies reserve these "cash cows" for in-house promotion of highly experienced managers who have earned their stripes, or in some cases, politically motivated promotions to "well-placed" people within the organization.

Size, Location, and "State" of the Office that You Are to Manage

In almost all instances, your first assignment with a multi-office company will be to take over an ailing branch office or to open a new one.

When interviewing with the company's upper management, you need to find out as quickly as possi-

In almost all instances, your first assignment with a multi-office company will be to take over an ailing branch office or to open a new one.

ble where and what your new assignment will be. Is it a new office based on good research, a mismanaged one, or one that was a bad idea from the start? This knowledge is critical to your success, both financial and reputation-wise, so don't commit to anything until you know all about the office that they want you to run. I took over an ailing branch office in California in the early nineties. I was the sixth manager in four years! It had seventeen of forty-four desks empty and was only averaging $2.2 million in monthly sales. I saw the potential, so I took the job. In ten months I had terminated six agents,

Carefully Consider the Following:

- What is the physical condition of the office and equipment?
- Will the company refurbish the office if necessary?
- What is the company's reputation in the brokerage community and why?
- How well located is it?
- Is the company willing to relocate the office if necessary?
- What is the office's main marketing area?
- Is the company's reputation a good fit for that marketing area?
- What is the makeup of the sales staff and the administrative staff? (I've seen a belligerent administrative staff tear an office apart.)
- How many agents will the office accommodate?
- How many empty desks and non-productive agents are there?
- Are there "factions" or splinter groups that have formed in the office? Who are the "players," and how will you deal with them?

hired thirty-four new ones, and increased the sales volume to over $7 million per month. Needless to say, I walked on water as far as the owners were concerned.

Company's Philosophy Versus Yours

A management position is hopefully a long-term thing. If you are going to spend a considerable amount of your time with a company, it is important to know that your philosophy (that is, your ideals, aspirations, methods, ethics, and the overall way that you do business) is compatible with that of the owners or upper management of the company.

During your interview with upper management it is best to make yourself a checklist regarding any and all of these matters, and discuss them thoroughly with the people that you will be working for. These things may include:

- How much latitude will you have regarding hiring and firing? This applies to both the administrative staff as well as the sales staff.

- How long will you have to get the office profitable?

- What is their philosophy on recruiting "incentives" to experienced agents, and if they offer any, will they stand by them indefinitely? If you are offered some type of incentive on an indefinite basis and the company takes it away six months later, you have a problem.

- Will they back you up in your decisions to terminate popular, but unproductive, agents (the ones that water the flowers, help plan the parties, and so on, but never sell anything)? You must not tolerate these people.

- Is their attitude toward marketing and recruiting highly aggressive or laid-back?

If you are a good recruiter, you are fairly aggressive at "soft-selling" the company on a consistent basis to good, experienced agents. If the company's attitude is more laid back, management may not see the need to give you the recruiting budget that you feel you need. However, if they expect you to recruit a large number of experienced agents in a short time in an area where the average tenure of good agents is several years with the same company, you have a problem, so work it out up front.

Methods of Compensation and Benefits

A discussion of compensation and benefits can be found in Chapter One. Quickly restated, the methods of compensation for selling managers and non-selling managers vary a great deal.

Selling managers are most often paid via a salary, which should be negotiated up front, prior to accepting the position. (NOTE: Don't be afraid to negotiate with the company on salary.) Management's offer is very often subject to negotiation. If they like you, they will just say no to any excessive demand on your part and stand pat on their offer. They won't automatically look for another person. Many will even like your spunk!

. . . the methods of compensation for selling managers and non-selling managers vary a great deal.

Beyond the salary, health (and sometimes dental) insurance is usually offered to the company's employees (you will be an employee). You can also make good money in bonuses. The companies that I have worked for have paid bonuses in several different ways. One example is 2 percent of the company dollar paid monthly (company dollar is gross income minus salespersons' commissions), plus 10 percent of the net profits paid semiannually. For the right office, these bonuses can easily equal or exceed your salary.

If you are opening a new office, or taking over one in need of good new agents, recruiting is the most important job at hand, so ask for a recruiting bonus as previously stated. Be ready to explain the benefit of that type of incentive to the company since it greatly increases your desire to make and keep it a priority and is a one-time payment for a long-term income stream. NOTE: Above all, do not show any embarrassment regarding what you ask for! You are the catalyst that will make or break the operation.

> NOTE: Above all, do not show any embarrassment regarding what you ask for! You are the catalyst that will make or break the operation.

A selling manager often gets a 5 to 10 percent increase in his or her commission split, but not always. As stated before, this type of increase often acts as a disincentive to perform your management duties because of the greater financial rewards of selling, so be very careful to balance your time carefully if this is a part of your compensation package.

If you have a large client base that you do not want to lose, you will probably want to reserve the right to sell to them, even if you are a "non-selling" manager. A large, loyal client base is a very valuable thing to have and giving it up should not be undertaken lightly.

Chances for Advancement

Most real estate companies are not structured very deep vertically. By that I mean that there simply aren't very many levels of management.

Most start with the office manager, then go up to a regional manager or area manager, then to some type of titled position such as president, northern California region, or president, western United States. Anything beyond that level will almost always involve an equity position in the company.

In light of this type of structure, there is not much room at the top, so in most instances you stand a better chance of advancement by acquiring a position within the same company, or being recruited by another company to take on a bigger and better office, or even more than one office. If you are asked to take on a second office for the same company, carefully evaluate the overall situation just as you did when you took on the first office.

If you are asked to take on a second office for the same company, carefully evaluate the overall situation just as you did when you took on the first office.

In addition, think about the distance between the two offices, the effect on your existing sales staff, and whether or not you would be flirting with burnout after a short time due to the possible overload on your time. If it is a new or existing "satellite" operation that is or will be very close to your existing office and won't take a huge amount of time, it's probably all right, but the "branch" agents can easily get the impression that they are the orphan child if you aren't around often enough, so be very careful about your decision to take on this type of situation. If it doesn't perform well, or if your main office shows signs of decline, it will probably be taken in a negative way by your boss. If you do take on that type of situation and make it run smoothly, it will position you for bigger and better things to come, such as a regional manager's position if one becomes available. I was promoted to regional manager with a large California firm in this manner, just prior to its purchase by a national conglomerate.

You will have to be patient and "earn your stripes." These bigger offices can be very lucrative financially and immensely challenging and rewarding from an operational standpoint. They are also fought for politically by the existing managers within a company, so if you want a promotion to a larger office, be prepared to present your case in detail to upper management as to why they should choose you.

"At-Will" Management Contracts

Unfortunately, many, if not most, manager's contracts are "at-will" contracts. This means that either you or the company may terminate the agreement (and the position) literally without notice. This can make you totally vulnerable to people with no integrity. As an example, you could be approached about managing an office that you had wanted to manage for years. It is in a wonderful location and has been a top performing real estate office for many, many years. During your interviews with the owner and senior management of that firm you are asked several times if you would manage another office within the company that really needed help instead of the one that you wanted. You declined every offer, saying that you were only interested in that particular office and would not take any other position.

You were then hired as the manager of the office that you wanted on the usual "at-will" contract and spent the next six months recruiting highly experienced agents, ending up with thirty people doing over $12 million volume per month. The owner was ecstatic with you, although he still couldn't find a manager for the ailing office in another part of town.

One of the major franchises is then purchased by a national holding company and a large real estate office near you is shut down. The manager of that office calls the owner of your company and says that he can bring nine good agents to "your" office if he is given the manager's position.

The next thing that you know, you are informed by voice mail that you have been replaced as the manager of that office and that, if you wanted to stay with the company, you could take over the ailing office.

Because of the "at-will" clause, you would have very little leverage, so, because you no longer wished to work for this company, you do your best to negotiate a "buy out" of your contract equal to maybe two months' salary or whatever is appropriate. The lesson here is to avoid this type of contract if you can, or at least get a reasonable termination period.

What About Your Existing Clients and Customers?

If you are opening your own company you will definitely need to maintain an active role in serving your clients and obtaining new business. You will also need to leave a certain amount of your earned commissions in the company checking account the first year. In 1975, my first full year as the owner of my own company, I grossed almost $60,000 but only took $32,000 home. The rest went to pay bills until I hired and trained a sufficient number of agents to produce a cash flow.

If you are opening or taking over a branch as a manager for another company, you will need to set the stage right up front about what you will and will not be allowed to do in servicing your existing clients and your ability to seek new ones. Get this in writing in your employment contract, including your commission split, so that no problems develop at a later date about the time that you spend with your own clients, if you are allowed to do that at all.

Opening Your Own Firm

Check the Demographics (Know Your Competition)!

Is there room for you to open your own firm or a branch office in the area that you have chosen? The only sure way to find out is to do all the necessary research and analysis prior to making any commitments. You must know the total amount of business available per year as well as how many firms are already absorbing it in order to assess your chances of success in penetrating any given market.

The old saying that "excess profits breed ruinous competition" is highly appropriate to the real estate brokerage profession. Most lucrative real estate markets in the United States have already been saturated, or are nearly so, by various sizes and types of real estate companies, including the national conglomerates. This doesn't mean that you are too late; it just means that you need to know what your staying power must be prior to making commitments.

Your best bet is to really know your market. If you are currently working in the market that you want to open an office in, you will no doubt have a reasonably accurate assessment of who the players are and how much room for you there will be. Regardless of how well you think that you know your target market, get at least three years worth of sales data from the Multiple Listing Service, if available, and thoroughly check the list on the following page.

- How many total units of sale were there each year?

- How many offices are "players" in your market?

- What is the average company dollar per sale? (The average company dollar is the gross commission to your office on the average sale price of a home in your marketing area, less the average commission paid to an agent in your office).

- What are your monthly operating expenses plus a reasonable profit? The National Realty Trust (NRT) currently will not keep an office open that cannot maintain a profit margin of at least 8 percent of gross revenues.

- How many average units must your office sell each month to achieve the desired result?

- Is there enough excess business available in units to allow your office to survive? If not, how will you take it away from the competition? It can be done!

- Who are the dominant agencies?

- Who are the dominant agents?

- Can they be recruited to your office?

- How seasonal is the sales activity?

- How much business is lost to out-of-area brokers?

- Is there an office that can be purchased more economically than opening a new one? This is often the case.

- Is the area prospering, static, or declining?

- Is there any good office space available?

- Are there any new, large subdivisions going in nearby that could take buyers away from the local resale market or be tapped for resale listings?

- Is there commission cutting going on?

- Check with the local Chamber of Commerce regarding any major employers that may be moving in or out of the area soon.

How Much Money Will You Need (the Business Plan)?

You will need both an analytical and a pro-forma business plan. The analytical business plan deals with where your office or company is, and where you want it to be in a given amount of time. The pro-forma business plan is a realistic model of where you expect your office or company to be in a given amount of time expressed in dollars and cents. See Appendix A for a model business plan. (Remember, most companies that fail do so because they are undercapitalized.)

(Remember, most companies that fail do so because they are undercapitalized.)

Why is a business plan so important? Like a highway map, the business plan acts as a guide along the way. It lets you know how you are doing as compared to what you thought was reasonable progress when you first started. It also lets you analyze where your strengths and weaknesses are and helps you direct your financial and personnel resources to their maximum advantage. If you are financing the start-up of your new office, your lender will require you to submit a detailed business plan prior to making any type of loan to you. Most business plans should be for at least five years. A good business plan will take many, many hours of exhaustive research and analysis to be an effective tool. Plan to create it and

A good business plan will take many, many hours of exhaustive research and analysis to be an effective tool.

Some Sources of Capital to Start a New Real Estate Office Are:

- SBA loans (see your local banker).
- Unsecured personal loans.
- Personal savings.
- Loans secured by your real estate, personal property, or retirement plans.
- Loans from family members, which may include a minority interest in the firm.

THIS MONEY IS PRECIOUS, SO BE CAREFUL AND PLAN WELL!

critique it several times before you have the finished product. Be very conservative and don't let your ego get in the way of good judgment.

Should You Buy a Franchise?

This is a highly personal decision and often depends on the market that you intend to open up in. While there are certainly exceptions, many of the franchises have never caught on in the upscale markets, even though some of the sales agents working for them have. Most franchises are strong in the start-up and mid-range markets.

The advantages of a franchise are: (1) immediate name recognition, (2) availability of training, (3) referral business (sometimes good, sometimes not), (4) purchasing power, (5) lower-cost errors & omissions insurance, and (6) high visibility via television commercials and generalized marketing materials.

The disadvantages of a franchise are: (1) overselling of franchises in a given area; (2) negative name recognition (a poorly run franchise office in your area can be assumed to be yours); (3) it is easier for your salespeople to use your franchise name successes to their own advantage if they open their own franchise firm in the same area; (4) franchise fees, which can run as high as 8 percent of your gross income; and (5) a preexisting reputation that a certain type of franchise just doesn't work in your market, which can make recruiting more difficult.

I bought and made excellent use of two franchises in the seventies and early eighties. It was the right vehicle for the lower-priced market where I opened my offices. Over the several years that followed, my biggest competitors were my own salespeople that left to open their own franchises in the same market.

Partnerships and Ownership Types

My observation of partnerships over the years has taught me that, almost without exception, they fail. It is like a marriage of two people that have no business being married to one another. Partnerships usually start with a person deciding to open his or her own firm, but lacking the financial resources to sustain the operation through its start-up phase, finds it necessary to bring in a partner. A few of these have actually worked, such as the highly successful

ERA franchise operation in San Bruno, California, where two experienced independents successfully merged into a large, multi-owner franchise operation with a big and sustained market share, but in my thirty years as a real estate professional, I have witnessed an overwhelming number of failures versus successes.

My advice is to think it through very carefully prior to taking on a partner, knowing that a few work and a lot don't. If you do take on a partner, I cannot stress enough the importance of having an attorney draft a written partnership agreement that all of the partners should agree to and sign before anything else takes place.

> *. . . think it through very carefully prior to taking on a partner, knowing that a few work and a lot don't.*

If you open or take over a branch office for another firm you will be an employee of that company and its ownership style will have little, if any, effect on you; however, there are several ways to "own" your own company that will give your personal assets some or total insulation from legal issues. **You should absolutely seek legal advice regarding this matter.**

The C corporation is a completely separate entity that you control, depending on how much of the stock you own. The state real estate departments require that your corporation, as well as you, be licensed as a real estate broker. This type of ownership can, if done right, offer a lot of protection of your personal assets, but there are stringent bookkeeping and other requirements needed in order to maintain legal and tax separation from your personal assets.

The S corporation is similar to a C corporation; however, profits and losses can flow directly through to the shareholders. It may or may not have as much insulation from legal claims as a C corporation, so check with your legal advisor.

A Limited Liability Company (or L.L.C., as it is commonly known) is a very popular way to own controlling interest in a real estate company today as it affords much of the same limitations on personal liability as a C corporation, but is far easier to set up and maintain. Some states do not allow real estate firms to be set up as L.L.C.s, so again, be sure to check with your tax and/or legal counsel prior to setting anything in place.

Many real estate companies are simply set up as sole proprietorships. This is the least costly way to operate but maximizes the exposure of your personal assets to legal claims and allows for no tax planning devices, as do most corporations and L.L.C.s.

Getting Started

Obtaining Office Space

Finding the right location is a critical step in setting up your operation. Your philosophy about what image you want to send to the public, as well as to the agents that you want to work for you, in a specific area, will determine what type of office space you obtain, how much space you obtain, and how you furnish it. Your demographic research will dictate how large an office you set up.

> *Finding the right location is a critical step in setting up your operation.*

Location

Neighborhood shopping centers are excellent office spots, provided they are flourishing and in good repair; however, as the average size of a real estate office grows, the need for parking can become so large as to create problems for other tenants in the center, and the rent of these offices is sometimes not conducive to a real estate operation. Do not ever get involved in a percentage lease as it will drain far too much of your net profits. A percentage lease is where you pay a base rent against a predetermined percentage of your gross revenue. In a real estate operation, you keep so little of the gross income that a percentage could ruin you financially.

Closed down restaurants or other buildings on shopping center pads can be excellent locations. Don't be afraid to bargain hard for these types of locations as there is often limited demand for them and they can remain empty for extended periods of time. The shopping center owners know this and should be ready to make considerable concessions to you. There are, of course, exceptions.

Freestanding office buildings are probably the best locations for real estate offices. Ground floor locations are the best, but are not absolutely necessary. If you can get good, visible signage and a second floor location with ample parking near the middle of your target market area, this is also an ideal situation.

Tenant Improvements

Tenant improvements can cost thousands of dollars. They are a part of any lease that you will sign and will either be calculated and added to the cost of the lease or partially or fully given to you as an incentive to sign a lease.

Negotiate hard regarding these improvements and get as much for free as you can. How hard you can negotiate will depend on the condition of the rental market (supply and demand) and how in demand the space is that you are negotiating for at the time.

Furniture, Equipment, and Supplies

The most precious commodity that you possess at this point is your cash reserves. It is very wise to use as little cash as you can to obtain furniture, equipment, and supplies. You should consult your accountant about the merits of leasing versus buying; however, if you do buy, finance as much as you can to conserve your cash.

Most real estate offices currently use the open area with cubicles, with a private office for the manager, an administrative area, and one or more conference rooms. This is very acceptable in nearly every marketplace. Some offices have private offices for top-performers. You will need to find out what your competition has for offices and make yours as good or better. Don't skimp on the quality of the furniture as it makes the office take on an entirely different feel. There is no need to be extravagant unless your market calls for it, but don't put in cheap-looking furniture and expect good agents to come knocking at your door.

If you want to attract good agents, put in good-sized cubicles with an ample work area and a two-drawer lateral filing cabinet. You should also have a dedicated phone line and an electrical outlet at each cubicle. The number of agents that use a computer at their workstation is growing exponentially; therefore, you must allow for it. You will not pay for an agent's phone line; just have it in place so that he or she can activate it if desired.

I highly recommend using portable or movable partitions. They are expensive, but they are yours and, if you move or reconfigure the office, you can take them with you or adjust their location.

They also come with built-in electrical outlets, which means that you will only have to stub out the electrical hookups here and there on the floor to be able to hook into the partitions as you assemble them.

Part of the process of signing your lease is deciding how many agents you want. This will also dictate the number of partitions, lateral file cabinets, and desk chairs that you will need, including a desk set for you and a conference table(s) and chairs.

You Will Also Need to Purchase:

1. At least one high-speed copier, with contingent plans for a second one after you employ forty agents.

2. One plain paper fax machine. You will need two later, one for incoming faxes that should be controlled by the listing/escrow secretary during business hours, and one for outgoing faxes with full agent access at all times.

3. One computer for approximately every fifteen agents equipped with MLS, Internet access, and word processing at a minimum. Set a policy from day one that no agent data is to be stored on the hard drives and must be stored to a disk. Let the agents know that your staff will check and erase any personal data from the hard drive monthly.

4. I recommend that you buy or lease a combination telephone/ voice mail system that can be added onto as your office grows. You will also need a computer for the manager, the administrative assistant, the listing/escrow secretary, and the floor desk.

5. A real estate office administration computer program purchased up front will be an excellent and relatively inexpensive investment and will allow you to easily track income, expenses, escrows, listings, and agent productivity.

6. You should also purchase a scanner and tie it in to one of the computers to be used by the agents.

7. You will need one paper cutter.

8. The only desks that you will need to purchase are for you and the administrative people, and you may circumvent the purchase of some of them by other means similar to the workstation modules purchased for the agents.

9. Budget for at least a five-month supply of stationery, envelopes of all sizes, the first set of business cards for each new agent hired, and a slush fund for "office products" such as pens, pencils, rulers, paper clips, three-hole punch, file folders, and so on.

10. One standard electric typewriter.

11. Computerized County tax records, such as MetroScan.

12. Postage machine.

Errors & Omissions Insurance

Once you hire that first salesperson, you have become legally liable for the acts of another person and you can be sued because of that person's conduct. I can't stress this enough, get good legal advice *before* you open for business.

Unless you are a branch manager, you *will* be named in any litigation against any of your sales staff while they are working for you, so protect yourself as fully as you can. There are many ways of obtaining legal protection from litigation against you. One is to form a Limited Liability Company, or L.L.C., if allowed in your state. Incorporating is another good way to limit your exposure. If operated right, either form of company ownership can drastically limit the legal exposure of your personal assets to judgments from a court.

It is also a *must* that you obtain Errors & Omissions insurance to cover you and each of your sales staff. They should be made to pay for their own insurance as a normal part of doing business. Costs and coverage vary widely, so obtain several different quotes, read them over carefully, and then decide which plan works best for you. A plan with *tail coverage* is the best one to have as it continues to cover an agent even after he or she no longer works for you. *Be sure to discuss this matter with your attorney after you have reviewed each policy yourself and made notes.*

Hiring the Administrative Staff

You will have a limited budget during the initial stages of your new company's operation and the administrative assistant that you hire will almost surely have to do multiple tasks during the first few months of operation. The same will probably apply with a company's new branch office.

Although the sales staff will be independent contractors, your administrative staff will be employees and will be subject to a different set of rules than the sales staff. You need to be careful here. The administrative assistant needs to be very loyal, eager to help you and the new agents, and compatible with your personality. If friction develops between you and the administrative assistant, the sales staff and potential new recruits will feel it, which is not conducive to the kind of supportive atmosphere that must prevail in a sales office.

Take your time and interview several people before making a decision. Ask them about their previous or current position, and what they like and don't like about it. Why are they considering leaving? What do they expect from their employer? What type of relevant experience do they have? What are their three best and three worst traits? How much are they making now? Make yourself a checklist of these and other questions to use during all interviews.

Above all, *ask for, and check, references.* Even if someone sparkles above the rest of the candidates, check him or her out thoroughly. Never hire someone the same day. Control the interview by asking "open-ended" questions: Why are you. . .? How do you feel about. . .? Is there a reason that you couldn't. . .? What do you think about. . .? Tell me about. . .are just a few of the open-ended type of questions that will elicit potential employees' feelings and personality about various things. Don't make the mistake of talking too much yourself while trying to sell them on your company. That can come later, after you've decided that you want to hire them. The individuals are obviously interested or they wouldn't be there.

Let's stop a minute to remember a very important point. We, as real estate agents, aspire to equal rights for all people, so it is a given that you must adhere completely to the Equal Employment Opportunity Act mandated by the federal government. It is not only the law, it's just plain fair. A person's race or religious or ethnic background, nor any of the other protected issues under that act, have anything to do with how well he or she will perform a job, so play it straight with people. It's what we are all about, and you'll open your doors to a lot more highly qualified applicants.

You should use the popular "at-will" contract with all of your employees so that if someone doesn't work out you can separate him or her from the company with the least amount of hassle or possibility of legal ramifications. This is, of course, just the opposite of what I said earlier about you negotiating an "at-will" contract with your employer if you hire on as a branch manager, but you're wearing a different hat now and have to act in your own best interests.

After you hire the administrative assistant, allow him or her to act as the initial contact for any further employee hiring. When you grow enough to need additional help (such as an escrow/listing secretary or a receptionist, for instance), explain the position to your administrative assistant carefully. Give him or her a list of questions to ask and let him or her screen all applicants before you meet with them. This is good time management and allows the "AA" to feel as though he or she is a part of the decision-making process and somewhat empowered.

Each person that you hire *must* sign a written employment agreement. Ask your attorney to draft one for you that both of you are comfortable with.

Cross-Training

I cannot stress enough how important it is to cross-train each new staff member into all of the positions that are available in your company. Let your employees become proficient in the position that they were hired specifically for first, then, as they mature, assign them to work an hour per day at the next position up the ladder until they are comfortable with most of it. This serves two purposes: It gives you flexibility and continuity in the event of an employee's absence and it gives the employees less bargaining power with you.

Cross-train each new staff member into all of the positions that are available in your company.

Be sure that it is in the employees' written job description that they are to cross-train at each position to your reasonable satisfaction. This may seem like you are giving them skills that they can take elsewhere in the marketplace if there isn't room to grow at your company, but if they want to be promoted, they will watch the other people anyway while they are doing their own job and, after they feel confident enough, they will leave. If you cross-train them, it gives them a sense of being next in line for the higher position.

The rest is up to you to maintain a work environment that makes them want to stay.

Quarterly Reviews

You should plan to meet with your staff quarterly to review their job performance. Using their job description as a guide, prepare a questionnaire listing their duties, with additional space for such things as attitude, resourcefulness, interaction with others, and any other items that you feel are important to you. Give them a copy of the questionnaire and have them fill it out and give it back to you at least two days prior to your review meeting. It should be designed so that they rate themselves in one column and you rate them in a second column. The reason for this is that you work very closely with these people every day and it can become very uncomfortable to start talking about a perceived problem that you have with something that they are not doing correctly, or other various behavioral situations (e.g., too many smoke breaks, arriving late, leaving early, talking too much, too many personal calls, and so on).

If you use a checklist, the employees must address it first and are often more critical about it than you may have been. The form should have a pre-printed area where each job function is listed, with an area next to it for a rating mark of some type, such as 0–10 with 10 being excellent. There should also be blank spaces where you can write in items as previously mentioned.

You will find these meetings much more productive and less confrontational using this system.

Remember, always praise in public and criticize in private. No exceptions!

Remember, *always praise in public and criticize in private. No exceptions!*

Plan to individually meet quarterly with each member of your staff for a short one-on-one. If possible, this should be away from the office over lunch or coffee. This is one-on-one time and should be used to let the employee tell you about anything that's important to him or her, business or personal. Your role should be to listen carefully and acknowledge what you are told, then offer suggestions or advice. If advice is offered about a situation in the office and you say that you'll act on it, be sure to do so if appropriate. If you don't, the employees will see little reason to meet with you. Believe me, their input about the goings-on in the office can be extremely helpful.

Pre-opening Promotional Advertising and Events

It is said that you only get one shot at a good first impression. That's pretty much true about opening a new real estate office, too.

You need to get the word out about your new firm to two different groups of people: the general public who will be your direct customers, and the agents in the area that you want to work for you. We will discuss promoting to the general public here and we will discuss the real estate agent group in the next chapter, "Recruiting."

You should definitely consider at least some type of newspaper display advertising. First, set a budget, and then have a meeting with the newspaper representatives. Remember that these people are usually on commission and get paid more for bigger ads, so do not let them talk you into more than you need.

At the meeting, tell them your budget, then ask them to come up with some ideas and get back to you. In preparation for this first meeting, you need to decide what type of image you want to send to the public—be ready to convey that to the newspaper representatives at your meeting. Do you want a big 100-person low-price range, high-volume business? Are you opening a small, 30-person boutique office dealing only in upscale properties, or something in-between? You only have so much money in the budget and *it has to count,* so this is a critical decision.

Remember: Everyone's favorite radio station is station WIIFM (or "What's In It For Me?"). All of your advertising dollars must sell benefits, not features, or they are ill spent and will bring you little or no results. Prior to your first meeting with the newspaper representatives, decide who your target market is, then ask yourself, "If I were a person in the market that I'm trying to reach, what would make me notice this company and want to do business with them?" Little catch phrases like "We care about you" or "We are a full service brokerage" have absolutely no meaning to the public because they don't have any benefit to them. Ads with statements like "Ask us about our written performance guarantee" or "We guarantee our work *in writing*" will go a lot further toward getting a customer to call you to see what that means. Be sure to tell your newspaper representatives about station WIIFM so that they can use that as a guideline for the ideas that they bring back to the table at your second meeting. If the representatives try to get you to exceed your budget for any reason, tell them that it is not open for discussion.

You do not necessarily have to use the big metropolitan newspaper. Most of the time its rates are usually higher, and the coverage is too broad for what you want anyway. There may be an "image" issue that you need to deal with that will force you to use the big paper, but if you do use one ask their representatives about special zone advertising that most have that costs much less money and will only cover the area that you want. The smaller local papers are actually quite well read and are usually an excellent medium in which to place your ads.

Plan on running either three or four *noticeable* ads, spaced a week apart. Even though they are a display ad, be sure that they are placed either in the real estate classified section or the business section and as near to the upper right corner of the page as possible. This is the most-read area of a newspaper page. Do not get "wordy." Your ad should convey in as few words as possible what your new office is about and how it benefits anyone in the community that wants to sell or buy. People will not stop to read a lengthy sales pitch and will actually dismiss your ad if it's too wordy.

Your last two ads should invite the public to your Grand Opening Celebration. Offer refreshments and a drawing for a television or something of that sort. That will bring in more people and get you some names and phone numbers to follow-up on. You should also send written invitations to all of the real estate agents that you would like to hire and, if you do have a drawing, have each of them drop a business card into the raffle box. Plan an Open House type forum, with the free TV drawing held between 4:00 to 7:00 P.M. Don't make it for too long or you'll only have a couple of people there at a time and they will feel uncomfortable. Send a courtesy note with the winner's name to each entrant for credibility. This is also an excellent lead in to see who's interested in moving.

Direct mail to the local neighborhoods around your new office location is also a highly effective way of getting the word out. Direct mail pieces should do the same thing as the classified ads; that is, say as much, with as few words, as possible. An image will stick in people's minds long after any words that they may have skimmed over. As with the newspaper ads, you might want to offer a Grand Opening Special, perhaps a free Home Warranty and Pest Control Report, or free appraisal fee, if customers present the ad or mailer to you at the time they list or sell with your firm for the remainder of the year or a certain number of months. Use light-green paper for your mailer and even border it to give it the connotation of money. After all, it is valuable and people will tend to keep it longer if it resembles money.

The best results are obtained by either mailing the flyer, then phoning the neighborhood's citizens to see if they got it, and then offering them a personal invitation; or by walking the area, handing out the flyers, and personally inviting everyone that you meet.

Most title or escrow companies, as well as your favorite loan broker, will be eager to help pay for all or part of the cost of the party in return for a chance to be there and meet people. Check to be sure that this is still allowable under the rules of the Real Estate Settlement and Procedures Act of 1974 (RESPA). Those rules clearly govern what can and cannot be paid for by a provider of ancillary real estate services such as mortgage, title, escrow, or insurance services on behalf of a real estate broker.

Selecting and Hiring a Branch Manager, Sales Manager, or Contracts Administrator

There is no right place to put this topic in this book, as the need to hire these people will arise at different times for each of you. Feel free to refer back here when the time comes.

Suppose you have been working hard. You have spent many long days and lots of evenings out with new agents helping them present their first offer or take their first listing. You are taking home the new sales contracts that they are generating and doing your very best to review and initial them within the time prescribed by the Department of Real Estate in your state. The agents that you have hired have become very effective in generating business and, although you are very proud of the success that your company or branch office has attained, it is beginning to be more than you can handle by yourself. You need help. What do you do?

If you are the owner of your own company, you need a branch manager or sales manager to assist you, depending on what your role is and the direction that you are taking your company. Let's define each one and talk about their respective duties and how they will help you to achieve even greater profits and success.

Branch Manager

If you are planning on expanding your company horizontally (that is, you plan on opening one or more branch offices with you assuming the role of Chief Executive Officer and/or General Manager), you will need a branch manager in each of your offices.

This person will be the point person in that branch and will be totally responsible for its overall successful operation. He or she will report directly to you and will be subject to your guidance and direct control. That person's duties will consist of hiring and supervising the administrative staff as required, recruiting new and experienced agents, controlling the operating budget within pre-set limitations, agent development, agent retention, providing counseling and guidance for the sales staff during their listing and sales efforts, and virtually everything that you currently do now. He or she will literally step into your shoes and run the office that you have developed.

Selection of this person is probably one of the most important "growth" issues that you will face. What should you look for in a branch manager?

1. A high level of maturity and experience. The candidate should be able to demonstrate, or has demonstrated by reputation, a high level of maturity in handling the day-to-day situations that arise during the operation of a real estate business. His or her ability as a top-performer is not nearly as crucial as the ability to think through situations, especially sensitive ones, and come up with sound, intelligent solutions that make sense to the agents as well as the clients involved. This person must possess technical skills as well as exceptional people skills and a mature, calm attitude toward problem solving.

2. Similar vision. This person must have similar values to yours. Not duplicate, just quite similar. You are still the catalyst of the organization and you want it to reflect your values, so hiring a branch manager that will uphold those values as you do is profoundly important. The people that currently work for you are there because they shared that vision with you. If a new manager stepped in with vastly different values, it could spell disaster.

You are still the catalyst of the organization and you want it to reflect your values, so hiring a branch manager that will uphold those values as you do is profoundly important.

3. A strong work ethic. A good manager and leader is often one of the first to arrive and often the last to leave at night. The new

manager must be highly motivated and willing to invest the time that is necessary to accomplish all of the many tasks that face him or her each day as well as be reasonably available, without question, when needed by a sales associate. He or she will be on stage with all of the sales associates watching, just like you were when you were the manager, and he or she must be willing to accept that responsibility.

Sales Manager

If you are planning on expanding vertically (that is, you are going to simply acquire additional space at your current office, or move to a different location and expand the size of your current operation), then you are in need of a sales manager, sometimes referred to as an assistant manager.

This person will be charged with whatever duties that you want to relinquish control of and give to him or her. Some of the usual ones are contract review, recruiting, training and agent counseling, and technical advice for the agents. You will retain whatever duties you feel are the most important ones to you. I strongly suggest that you stay involved with agent recruiting to a great degree as this activity has a great impact on the success of your business. As this person will have a big impact on the personality, and ultimately the success, of your office, the same values that are mentioned in the branch manager section are just as critical here.

Contracts Administrator

Effective budgetary and operational issues are leading more and more real estate companies toward "mega-offices" with 100 or more agents under one roof. The contracts administrator can serve as a highly effective part of your team both during your growth to a large office and as an integral part of your management team after you have achieved mega-office status.

Your office will grow to a point where you are too busy and maybe even overwhelmed with other administrative duties to be able to take the time to carefully review each contract as the Department of Real Estate demands. The last thing that you want to do is "skim" the contracts. This is a poor business practice and can spell trouble.

If you are in that position but really don't have the cash flow to pay a branch manager or sales manager yet, consider hiring a

Contracts Administrator. This person fulfills a very necessary duty and, because it is a limited duty, is usually not paid a large amount of money, often only several hundred dollars a month. They are still allowed to list and sell provided that they always review all contracts in a thorough and timely manner.

If you get to mega-office status and approach the level of 140 or more agents, you can make a good case for having both a branch or sales manager and a contracts administrator.

The contracts administrator's sole duty is to carefully read each listing and purchase contract that is generated by the sales staff and initial each one afterward within the time prescribed by your state Department of Real Estate. If he or she finds that documents are missing, especially timely or sensitive ones such as agency disclosure forms, lead-based paint disclosure forms, or ancillary services notification forms (title, loan, or other services that are owned or have a financial relationship with your company), he or she is charged with the responsibility of getting the agent to get them and turn them in. You should also be routinely notified if the contracts administrator is having trouble getting any of these forms.

The contracts administrator should also read all language put into the contract by the agents to see that it is clear as to the intent of the parties and that it cannot be interpreted in more than one way. If problematic contract issues are found, both you and the agent or agents involved should be immediately contacted so that a correction can be made if possible.

As the owner of the company or the designated broker, you will need to write a letter to the Department of Real Estate notifying them that the selected person has the authority to review and initial contracts on behalf of your company or a particular office within your company.

Recruiting

$\mathcal{A}$lmost without exception, every experienced manager will tell you this simple truth. There is no function that you can perform as an owner or manager of a real estate office that is as important to the quality and success of your office as recruiting highly motivated, quality agents. *There is no exception to this rule!*

> *There is no function that you can perform as an owner or manager of a real estate office that is as important to the quality and success of your office as recruiting highly motivated, quality agents. There is no exception to this rule!*

Suppose you have signed a lease for office space, bought or leased thousands (or even hundreds of thousands) of dollars worth of office equipment and furniture, probably hired an assistant, and made many other financial commitments. The reality is that someone needs to bring enough revenue in to pay for all of these things, and make you a profit. You probably can't do it alone, depending on what you have created and to what degree, so what do you do? *Start recruiting!*

There are two types of sales agents to select from: newly licensed agents with no experience, and experienced agents. Each group has their own set of advantages and challenges. In all likelihood, you will end up with a blend of both types of agents, and the percentage of each will be dictated to some extent by what you are all about and what the opportunities are in your marketplace. Let's take each type of agent and look them over.

New Agents

The two biggest advantages of hiring new agents are that they will be on a low commission split, giving you a higher "company dollar" share of the income that they produce (at least for awhile), and they also have great enthusiasm for the position and don't bring a lot of baggage with them. You can train them "your way" right from the beginning and teach them to do it right. While time consuming, this has many advantages.

When I opened my firm I hired all new agents since I wasn't well known. I absolutely lived with them, teaching them everything that I knew, and infecting them with my enthusiasm for the business. I specifically looked for highly motivated people that really wanted to use the opportunity well. You know, the type that couldn't sit still in their chair during the interview. I turned down many agents, that I felt were either just looking for a better commission split, but had no energy or anything else to offer in return, or new people that just didn't impress me as being go-getters. This patience paid off handsomely for me as I built an energy level in the office that was totally contagious and was greater than the sum of the parts.

The biggest disadvantages of new agents are that they don't really know what they are doing and, if you are not careful, they can get you and themselves in trouble. If you hire new agents, you must be willing to devote many, many hours of personal training and guidance to them. You simply owe them that and have taken on that responsibility and commitment when you hired them. You also have a responsibility to the general public who these people will be representing. They have a right to *Set a high standard and do not deviate from it—ever.* sound, professional guidance and representation. If you have new agents out there with the public, you need to be right behind them every step of the way until they mature to a certain level of competency. This also applies to many "experienced agents" that you may hire that weren't properly trained at their previous company. Be firm about this. Set a high standard and do not deviate from it—ever.

New agents are best recruited by small newspaper ads, visits to the local license training schools as a guest speaker, past clients, and speaking engagements at the business and/or real estate classes at your local colleges or universities.

Newspaper ads bring a varied group of people to you. You will talk to and meet with a whole cross-section of people, from the person that wants to sell his or her own home and thinks this is a way to reduce the commission, to the shining star that I mentioned earlier that is so motivated that he or she can't sit still in the chair. Keep your ad short. Ads can be very expensive, depending on the newspaper used. Use words like "high quality," "seeking a career with huge rewards," and other phrases that get their attention and make them want to call you.

I always had excellent luck in getting new agents by speaking at the license training schools. You simply call and tell them that you are a newer firm in town and are looking for high-quality new agents, and ask to be a guest speaker at one of their classes. These schools want to have a good placement record and are usually very obliging.

Take a quality handout with you. *Remember,* you only get one chance at a good first impression. Don't skimp and take some photo- copied thing that says "cheap" all over it. Take the time to develop a high-quality recruiting brochure to hand out. It should have graphics that give word pictures about what your firm is all about and should list several of the benefits to prospective agents of affiliating with your firm, such as security, training, reputation, location, office amenities, affiliation with relocation companies, and so on. Remember, the things that I just listed are features and you must state them, but then follow-up with why they are a benefit to the person reading the brochure or they are meaningless. Remember radio station WIIFM.

Remember, you only get one chance at a good first impression.

The training school will usually put you on near or at the end of the class, which is good. Give a short motivational talk about your firm, and then ask for questions from the audience. This creates an easy one-on-one dialogue and gives you the opportunity to tell them that you'll be glad to stay after class to speak to them privately. This is probably the single most effective method of recruiting new salespeople. *Caution:* Don't commit to hire anyone at the school. Just get the appointment to meet at your office. You will need to do some checking up before you hire anyone.

The essence of your talk should be about who you are; what compelled you to open your own firm or take on the new branch office that you manage; what you hope to achieve; and how they, as new agents, fit into your plans. Expect training to be one of the topics that will come up the most. If you are asked directly what your commission split is, simply say that it is progressive (meaning higher splits for higher earnings) and is set at the time of hiring. Do not get baited into having to defend your commission split at one of these meetings. An offer of tuition reimbursement with their first commission check is an excellent incentive.

Past Clients

If you have been in the real estate business for awhile and have a good enough client base, you should take the time to reflect on each of your past clients. If you feel that any of them would be good as a real estate agent, call these people and tell them what you are doing, that you feel that they would be a wonderful addition to your firm, and try to set up a meeting with them. Depending on what they are currently doing and what their motivation is, you could end up with an excellent agent. Your credibility is already established with them and they already know something about your style. I have hired several of my past clients over the years and it has always been a good experience.

College Business or Real Estate Classes

There is a huge amount of fresh, young talent eagerly awaiting a chance to enter the business world at every college or university. Many, if not a majority, of these people have not decided where in the business world they will focus their efforts. Call or visit the college and ask to speak to someone in the placement office. State the opportunities that you have available and ask if someone can help you get an appointment as a guest speaker at one or more of the classes. Although this is a different group from the real estate license school and may not be as focused on real estate as a career, many people just never considered it and may be intrigued. They are usually young, highly educated and motivated, and often make excellent agents. Follow the same guidelines for your speech that are stated in the licensing school paragraph.

Experienced Agents

Unlike new agents, experienced agents have a certain amount of "street smarts" and, depending on their tenure and where they are coming from, they will have a client base that they bring with them. There are two main advantages to hiring an experienced agent over a new one. Experienced agents are productive much faster (in many cases immediately) and therefore bring in revenue faster. Depending on their reputation, they may also help you to induce other agents to come work for you. The main drawback to hiring experienced agents is that they often want commission split concessions from you that are not very attractive to you. They may have also developed a bad work ethic. This is something that you must evaluate on a case-by-case basis before making a hiring decision.

If you have a Grand Opening Party, you need to make a decision on whether to invite all agents in any given office to attend or to selectively invite only agents that you have targeted as people that you would like to have working for you because of their reputation and production. If you invite only some people from an office you run the risk of offending the others; however, if they aren't worth having as agents anyway, there isn't too much downside.

If you are opening a brand new office, you will want to start your recruiting efforts at least two months prior to opening. You must first obtain a roster from your local board or association. Sit down and study it. Highlight every agent that you would like to have work for you. Set a time aside every day, call as many of these agents as you can, briefly tell them what you are doing, and ask if they can get together with you over a cup of coffee or lunch. The reason for this is that many of them are too busy for lunch but will take the time for coffee if they are at all curious about your new office.

If you are opening a brand new office, you will want to start your recruiting efforts at least two months prior to opening.

Prior to your first meeting with someone, you should have made a recruiting manual (that is, a manual that has an original of your new business cards, stationery and envelopes, and any marketing brochures that you will be making available). If you are offering something especially nice, like glossy brochures or a company-paid escrow coordinator, be sure to take the feature and say in writing what the benefit of it is.

When you meet, make enough small talk to get comfortable, but be aware of any time constraints the prospect may have. Begin the meeting by stating where you are opening your office and why you decided to make the move. Talk about your vision of where you see your company going and the added benefits of adding someone like your interviewee to the mix. Discussing things like how much market share you intend to capture, what markets you intend to focus on and dominate, what your office will look like, the amount and type of people you will allow to join your firm, and other interesting features can help convey where you are headed. On many occasions I have actually seen an agent pause at one of these meetings, smile, and say how good it sounds. This is the time to let your enthusiasm show.

You *will* be asked about commission splits, so it's best to be prepared for the question during the interview. I normally handle it by asking the agent what he or she made the previous year, or to date this year. I can then bring out my commission schedule and show where he or she would fit in. Since these figures adjust each year to some degree, I don't have a problem with making adjustments based on the individual's performance. Ask open-ended questions that can't be answered yes or no. The answer to "What interests you about my new company?" will provide more information than asking someone, "So, will you come work for me?" At some point, you will need to ask for a commitment if you want one. Use your own style in doing this, but don't end the meeting without asking the question. If your prospect is not yet ready to commit at that time, that's fine. Just keep in touch as often as you think is reasonable.

If a person says yes to your invitation (and many will), your next step should then be to ask if he or she knows of anyone else that might be interested in moving to your office. Quite often, agents make it a priority to help recruit once they hire on at a company. Always remember to thank these agents and show your appreciation for their help. A free car wash or a coupon book for Starbucks Coffee goes over extremely well and doesn't cost much, especially considering the help in recruitment.

At least quarterly, I ask all of the agents to bring a business card to the office meeting. At the meeting I ask them to write down the name and phone number of at least one good agent from another company that they would like to see working at our office. I then write a letter to those agents, telling them what I did and how popular they are with my staff, and that I'll call them in a couple of days to see if they have time for lunch or coffee with me next week. This has proven to be the start of many slowly formed, long-term relationships that eventually ended with the agent transferring to my office.

If your Multiple Listing Service, Real Estate Board, or Association has a weekly caravan or tour, you should always attend. It is an excellent time to greet agents and set up meetings. Most MLS caravans start with a general meeting. Arrive early, but don't sit down. Stand until some agents that you want to recruit come in, then go over and say hello. Ask where they are sitting and, if appropriate, sit with them. Ask them if they have heard that you are opening your own firm, or a new branch office. Whatever the answer, tell them that you feel that they are exactly the type of high-quality agent that you are looking for and that you would like to have lunch or coffee in the next few days to tell them more about the office. Ask for the meeting, and then let it go unless they want to know more right then.

During the time that you are out previewing the new listings on the MLS tour, you will get plenty of opportunities for a short chat with prospective recruits, most of whom you will already know. Don't hesitate to ask if they have heard about your new office, but don't try to get into too long a conversation about it there and then. Most agents are on a time schedule during caravan and will get anxious if you detain them too long. Just ask if you can call them for coffee or lunch and let it go at that unless you see that they want to stay and talk. Always have your recruiting manual in your car when you are on caravan. Sometimes you will meet someone near lunch and if you ask him or her, he or she will have lunch with you.

When you get within a month of opening, and from that day on, you must discipline yourself to cold-call agents every day. A computerized database like TOP PRODUCER, Agent 2000, or a couple of others is the best way to keep track of what you are doing and who you are talking to. It is extremely important that you keep good notes about each call that you make and when you make it.

First, make a contact-type database titled "Recruiting." Enter each agent that you want to hire in your database. Start by sending around ten letters a day out to your database. Tell these prospects in the letter that you are opening your own firm, or staffing a branch office, and that you have identified them as being among a small group of people that meet or exceed the standards that you have set in order to be hired by your firm. Say that you would like to meet with them for coffee or a quick lunch in the next few days to give them more details about what you are doing and that you'll call them in a day or two. Review what I said earlier about how the meeting should go. The important thing is to ask for a commitment if you feel that you still want to hire them. If they aren't ready yet, they'll let you know. "No" doesn't mean no permanently. Just keep in touch with them about once a month or so, depending on the individuals. Eventually something will happen at their company (a management change, a policy change, a conflict with another agent or the staff, or something else) to make them decide to move. If you've been in touch on a regular basis, you stand an excellent chance of getting them to hire on with you.

If, at your meeting, they agree to hire on with you as soon as you open, take the chance and spend the money for their business cards as soon as you can, even if it's well ahead of when they say they will move. When you get the cards, send them one in the mail and tell them that you have everything in place for them to maintain or increase their productivity.

That single item, fear of loss of productivity or "downtime," is the single biggest thing that keeps even unhappy agents where they are. You *must* stress to anyone who shows interest in your firm that you are prepared to do whatever is necessary to help maintain or increase his or her productivity. Really focus on this and it will pay you great dividends.

> *You must stress to anyone who shows interest in your firm that you are prepared to do whatever is necessary to help maintain or increase his or her productivity.*

Two of the most important things that you can do are to have their business cards and announcements ready for them when they arrive. A real plus is to make a part-time college person available to address their announcements for them either prior to, or right after, their move. They will love the thoughtfulness of this!

Once someone is on your recruiting list, stay in touch as often as you feel is reasonable. Some people may be very receptive to your offer and appear ready to move on—these people should be contacted weekly. However, others may be receptive to what you've said, but not yet ready to make a career change. These people may be better served with a monthly call, so you can gauge how they are feeling about their current situation. You need to individually evaluate your contacts, and determine when you will next contact them in your contact management program.

Every time you hire someone, especially someone who is a "good catch," send out a little note to the rest of the agents in your database and let them know. Follow with "only five (or however many) desks are still available. Can we meet?"

Above all, don't be worried about being a pest. The ones that really do not want to move will tell you so, and all of them will be flattered that you thought enough of them to ask, so *call consistently!*

> *Every time you hire an experienced agent from another firm, ask him or her who else at the prior office might benefit from moving to your office.*

Remember: Every time you hire an experienced agent from another firm, ask him or her who else at the prior office might benefit from moving to your office. This will often get you two or three good agents instead of only one, and all you had to do was ask!

Real Estate Association and Community Activities

The better known that you become in your real estate association, the better your chances are of having an experienced agent recognize you when you make a recruiting call. That will almost always lead to a longer, better dialogue and increase your chances of getting an appointment with him or her to talk about moving to your company. You will need to be careful about getting involved in committees that must make controversial decisions such as the grievance committee or the professional standards committee. It's very hard to endear yourself to an agent that you just slapped the hand of for an infraction of the association's rules or regulations. Conversely, becoming known for serving on these types of committees will almost always get you a reputation for having very high ethical standards yourself, which is attractive to all of the right agents.

Becoming involved in community activities such as local elected office or city and county boards, committees, and professional groups is another effective way to get yourself known, gain a reputation as a civic-minded person, and make it easier to connect with real estate sales agents.

Just remember, to do the job effectively will take a certain amount of your time, so be very careful that you have the time to invest in any position that you take and do it right. A reputation as a "no-show" will hurt you much more than it will help you.

Training

*A*s you amass your new sales force, you will have a highly vested interest in their level of competency. For reputation purposes as well as legal protection and proper representation of your firm's clients, you will need to begin a whole series of training sessions. Although your sales staff will in all likelihood be independent contractors whom you can't make attend training meetings, you can set a standard up front that

> *As you amass your new sales force, you will have a highly vested interest in their level of competency.*

anyone that you designate as needing training that doesn't elect to attend all training sessions offered and recommended by you will be terminated. Believe me, it's that important!

In-House Group Training

This type of training is mostly lecture; however, if you only have a small group of around eight to ten people, you can incorporate role-playing along with it. The role-playing must be realistic and, when done right, greatly adds to retention and understanding of the subject matter. If you are lecturing to a large group, role-playing becomes more difficult because of the lack of proximity of some group members to the speakers.

As with any meeting that you conduct, have a written agenda for your training session as well as a written guideline for the agents to follow and take notes on. When you really want to stress a point, say, "Be sure to write this down." You may want to follow a logical sequence in your training sessions. I start with the Purchase Agreement, or Deposit Receipt. This class takes me around three hours with a break in the middle. I go over every paragraph in it in detail and explain the ramifications of it. Most of my sessions, except for the Purchase Agreement, last an hour or less, but this one is so important and sensitive that I will not shorten it. It is very necessary to have a question and answer session after each of your sessions. This makes it easier for someone who didn't understand something to get clarification without being embarrassed. You will usually have to prompt the group for questions at first due to people's tendency to not want to speak in public, but after a couple of prompted questions and answers, the real issues will flow. These sessions are fun to do.

Other training sessions should include the listing agreement; presenting offers and counteroffers; presenting multiple offers; prospecting, including door-to-door, cold-calling, and mailing; legal issues; financing (bring in a lender as a guest speaker); Open House techniques; how to work with "for sale by owners"; time management; how to build a referral business; how to sell income property; and agent personal finances.

One very important issue about these meetings, as with all meetings, is to start and end exactly on time. Nothing says louder that you don't respect an agent's time like making him or her wait for stragglers or ignoring the end of session time.

Peer Group Training

Except for recruiting, this is by far the most effective way to quickly add to your net profit through the efforts of your sales staff.

Almost without exception, every real estate office has the same profile. There are usually two to four top producers that bring in about one-third of the gross revenue. The next 40 percent of the office bring in about 50 percent of the gross revenue and the remaining 45 percent of the agents bring in the remainder of the gross revenue, or about 17 to 20 percent.

Except for recruiting, this is by far the most effective way to quickly add to your net profit through the efforts of your sales staff.

Your first step must be to list each agent in order of gross revenue produced to the office, before any split. Then divide your office into revenue groups of one-third each. It will closely parallel the previous scenario. Your target is the second group. Starting at the bottom, you must "invite" each agent to join in a special self-improvement group of ten people. Tell each agent that you will be conducting several of these groups and you would like each to join you in the next one.

Once you get ten people, arrange for a one-hour meeting on a chosen day of the week. Go into a conference room or anywhere where there will be no distractions. Take the table out of the room if there is one there and line up eleven chairs around the edge of the room (one for each person and one for you, as the moderator). Above all, start and finish on time. Do not deviate from this.

At the first meeting, ask all the participants if they know what the word *commitment* really means. A little role-playing may help drive the point home. Select a participant that you know has children, and set up a situation where that person's child is lying unconscious on the kitchen floor next to an open bottle of poisonous stuff. Ask your participant "What would you do?" For every answer you receive, counter with a rebuttal. For example, if you're told, "I would get in the car and drive to the emergency room," you reply, "Your car won't start." If the suggestion is "I would call 911," counter with "Your phone is dead." If your partner states, "I would have the neighbors take me," answer that "They aren't home." Point out that the hospital is thirty blocks away. Ask your partner if he or she would gather up the child and run those thirty blocks if necessary. The answer, of course, will be yes. At that point, after you have role-played the issue enough to drive home your point about the "commitment" needed to get help for the child, explain to the group that the purpose of the exercise was to drive home what true commitment really is . . . a mindset that simply does not allow for failure.

That is the premise that you will build the training class on. You will ask them to "commit" in writing each week to at least one thing

> *Drive home what true commitment really is . . . a mindset that simply does not allow for failure.*

in each of three categories: business, personal, and health. After you explain what will go on, ask if anyone feels that he or she can't handle this for the next eight weeks. Excuse anyone that wants out (you'll deal with these people later).

Explain to the group that anyone not meeting his or her commitments the first time will be excused from the meeting for the remainder of that day and asked to go immediately and finish whatever it takes to meet the commitment. Anyone that fails to keep a commitment a second time will be dismissed from the program.

Be sure to emphasize that you are the moderator and it will be the other agents who have met their commitments that they will have to deal with if they don't. You *must* emphasize the importance of peer pressure as a deterrent to failure. Hand out a form that you have devised and ask them to fill it out right away. Many agents will use making a certain number of cold calls, or holding a certain number of Open Houses, or seeing a certain number of for sale by owners as their business commitment; such things as a certain number of minutes of exercise per day or a certain number of pounds lost or a good house cleaning as their personal commitment; and possibly a certain number of chapters in a book read or doing charity work for their personal commitment. *Caution:* It is extremely important that agents commit to things that they can fully control, such as the number of cold calls made, and not to things like take two listings, where their outcome depends on the acts of another.

The reason for positioning the chairs around the room is to accentuate the peer pressure. Each week, start the meeting at exactly the prescribed time. Ask everyone how they did, generally. Then go around the room, using your copy of last week's commitments, and ask each person to state his or her goals and what was done to achieve them. Applaud everyone that has successfully accomplished all the stated commitments. For those who have not fully achieved one or more commitments, demand to know why, and encourage the rest of the group to do likewise. In other words, take these agents to task and "get in their faces" as to why they did not complete what they committed to. Tell everyone that the group belongs to them, its effectiveness lies in all of them taking it seriously, and that they should take anyone who doesn't to task. The idea is to make not achieving commitments so uncomfortable that the group develops a mindset of achievement. It really works, but only if you hold the group up to a highly defined standard of commitment and do not take failure lightly.

At the end of the ten weeks, have a small prize for each member of the group that met all of his or her commitments. Remind them that they have all come a long way and that if they persist in this way of running their lives, they will not only be excellent real estate agents, but also will be winners in every area of their lives.

There are two major benefits from this type of training. One is that the people in the class really start to feel good about themselves. They slim down, feel better physically, gain a "winner" attitude, and become more productive in their business. To a person, their self-esteem improves. Many will ask if they can go through the class again. Tell them yes, later. You're on to a new group for now.

The second benefit is that the agents just above them in the earnings category will start to sit up and take notice that these people are now standing up at the office meetings and talking about their new listings or sales. They will feel somewhat threatened and some of them will actually ask you if they can be a part of your next group. They will "turn up the burner" and become more productive to keep their place in the order of things. This includes the top performers. The group below this group will either pick up on the momentum and better themselves to get into one of your classes or they will fire themselves and you won't have to. Remember, this will crumble around you and become a joke unless you set and enforce rigid standards and take people to task, including removal from the program, if they do not meet the self-set standards. It is also highly important that the other participants all know the power and necessity of peer pressure, and they freely use it.

Field Trainer

A field trainer is an experienced agent that takes a new agent under his or her wing and works with the new agent "in the field," with actual clients. In the beginning you will be the field trainer and will have to be extremely careful about your time management. If you are a branch manager on a salary and bonuses, it is far easier than if you have opened your own firm since you probably will not be listing and selling on your own. If it's your firm, you will still have to list and sell in order to pay the bills during your start-up time. The more new people that you hire and train, the more demands on your time there will be to go with them to present offers and take listings.

The object is to get new agents to a certain level of competence and confidence as soon as possible so that they no longer need you with them when they conduct listing and selling activities. Nothing will make this happen faster than personal one-on-one training from you, including realistic role-playing. That's how I got fifteen agents doing the huge volume of business that we did in Daly City in such a short time. Nothing pays greater dividends than the intense personal training of each new agent. It not only gets them productive faster and avoids burnout, but also sets their standard for what is a "normal" level of competence and daily activities for an agent. Remember, they will want to be just like you.

Nothing pays greater dividends than the intense personal training of each new agent.

Each person is different, and while some people will want you to go with them on several occasions and do most, if not all, of the talking while they just watch, others will only want to see you in action once or twice to feel comfortable. It is absolutely your call, and yours alone, as to when an agent is ready to go it alone, so be sure to explain that up front. At some point with each agent, you will go along but have very little to say and will only intervene if you see things going astray. Be sure and tell the agents what role you will play before you get to the appointment. Don't be afraid to let them make mistakes, but help keep them on track as necessary. As you watch them work, keep track of both positive and negative things as they occur. After the appointment is over, privately critique how they did. Be factual and benevolent about their strengths and weaknesses. Ask them how they might handle it differently the next time. This is good, solid, and effective training at its best. Bring up any successes of theirs, as appropriate, at your office meetings. Nothing builds confidence like public recognition for a job well done.

I personally never go with a new agent when he or she is showing property. This is best taught in a training class and role-played in advance of the first showing appointment. I do let the agent know that I will be on my cell phone if he or she *really* needs me, though. I usually try to plan my time around an agent's first showing so that I am at the office and available in case he or she writes an offer and needs any advice or moral support. Many agents are really scared about writing that first offer; if they know you'll be around, they are far more inclined to seek out and work with buyers. You need to give each agent assigned to you a daily activity list (that is, a minimum list of activities that he or she is to perform on a daily basis). Be realistic about this and remember that these agents will not be approaching these activities with the same level of competence or confidence that you would be. The activities should include: seeing all new office listings; some form of prospecting, which can include cold-calling, door knocking, and for sale by owners; and research, which should be both community-wide as well as specific, as in their chosen "farm area." This would include previewing new subdivisions or currently listed homes, and driving by homes that have sold, to become aware of property values; property analysis, which would include a written analysis of an assigned property every other day by you; and follow-up with current prospective sellers and showing property when they have buyers to work with. See Appendix B for a sample Agent Business Plan.

You should map out a full nine-hour day for them for each day as a standard to follow, including a day off. I have never believed that you have to work twelve-hour days on a continual basis to be successful, but you do have to make every minute of those nine hours count. Remind your agents that we do not sell property. We sell time and knowledge, and the more motivated people that they spend their time sharing their knowledge with, the more successful they will be. That is the essence of a top-performer!

All of the above means absolutely nothing unless you have a system for tracking agents' time and activities and holding them accountable. Again, you need to remember that they do not yet have your ability to do the most productive thing at any given moment. If you leave them on their own to figure it out, they are bound to pick up bad time management habits along the way.

When new agents are at the end of their training, or far along enough that you are allowing them to do some activities, pre-set a time for them to meet with you at least twice a week to review their performance and adherence to the activities that you have set for them to do. Question them on their knowledge of their farm area, if they have chosen one. Ask them to tell you about two or three new listings that have come into the office, and what for sale by owners they have visited and how those relationships are progressing. In other words, make them highly accountable for their time and the results that they achieve. Offer feedback and suggestions. If you do this regularly early in their career, they will develop this as a way of working and a standard by which they will measure themselves long after you have turned them loose, and you will both prosper greatly for it!

Remember, your job as a manager is to obtain predetermined results through the efforts of other people. This type of training combined with a high degree of accountability is at the very core of what a good manager is all about.

Remember, your job as a manager is to obtain predetermined results through the efforts of other people.

As your firm grows, ask some of the senior agents if they will consider being a field trainer. Some top-performers don't want to be bothered with new agent development; therefore, stick with good to top agents that have a nurturing personality type. They will be much more inclined to devote the time to properly help develop a new agent.

As compensation to the field trainer, I offer 15 percent off the top of each commission received by the office that was generated by the new agent while on the field training program. I charge the agent 5 percent and I pay 10 percent. This fee is paid for a minimum of two listings and two sales, and can only be changed by me. If I have a more aggressive agent that learns faster, I may cut him or her loose from the program sooner, or conversely, a more timid agent or slower learner may stay in the program longer. It is made clear that, with input from the field trainer, it is at my sole discretion as to when any particular agent is turned loose.

Role Playing

My observations over the past thirty years have overwhelmingly shown me that most people learn better and quicker by doing than by observing. Lecture certainly has its place in any type of training; however role-playing is by far the most productive and effective way to get someone to feel comfortable performing learned skills.

Role-playing is by far the most productive and effective way to get someone to feel comfortable performing learned skills.

I have had the greatest results over the years with small groups of one to four people. The reason for this is that, without exception, no one wants to be embarrassed in front of others. The larger the "observing" group is, the more intimidated each person is. As with any type of training, you are trying to impart how to handle various types of situations. This is best achieved if the group has a benchmark of effective conduct or ability to refer to. The group members respect you and want to be just like you, so if you show them an effective way to accomplish something first, by role-playing it with someone else, they will easily learn to emulate what you did and how you did it. Only after you have set the standard for the group should you assign them roles and get them actively involved.

Take any situation that you want to build their skill in and either ask one of your senior agents to role-play it with you first, or ask a member of the group to do it. Have them take the customer role while you take the agent's role. Provide a scenario of what is taking place first, such as asking a for sale by owner for a listing appointment, writing an offer on a home, presenting an offer or multiple offers, or cold-calling, then simply start a dialogue. It is important that the person acting as the customer is as realistic as possible and gives you the normal objections, without becoming overly aggressive or too easily persuaded. That's why it is often better to have it somewhat rehearsed with a senior agent first.

Once you have played out the situation, ask for feedback. Ask the group what you did wrong and what you did right. If you want you can blatantly do things wrong on purpose to stress a point. Ask them to tell you a better way to handle any problem areas.

After your performance is critiqued, assign the group roles and ask them to do the same thing. You can (and probably should) be the customer so that you can be sure to interject enough objections and obstacles without becoming too overbearing. Always have the group critique each performance immediately after it is completed so that strong points can be affirmed and problem areas can be addressed while they are still fresh in everyone's mind.

Don't overlook newer agents that come to work for you as candidates for role-playing skill sessions, as well as an experienced agent that is in a slump. I have hired many experienced agents over the years that became much more productive after going through some of these sessions. When that happens, they usually become an excellent recruiter for you. This is a great way to show off your skills, so don't be surprised if you get offers from several of your senior agents to help you out with these sessions, and don't be afraid to ask them to help. Most of them love the recognition and do a very good job.

Top-Performer Panels

These panels are usually lecture-type training sessions, but can be combined very effectively with role-playing as well. Just be sure that the panel is well prepared for whatever roles you have assigned them.

This type of training involves having a group of very experienced and successful agents sit in front of a large group of new or newer agents and explain how they became such top agents. This is a wonderful way to give recognition to your top producers and is a highly effective way of imparting well-founded knowledge and skills to a larger group of people.

To make this as effective as possible, give it a lot of publicity by handing out flyers to each of your agents and mentioning it at each of your sales meetings for about three weeks ahead of time. Have a sign-up sheet available and let your agents know that attendance by them is very important to you. This is also a wonderful time to invite agents from other companies that you are trying to recruit.

The session should last for two to three hours, with a break at the halfway point. An effective format is to have each of the three to five top producers speak for twenty minutes about what they do and why they do it, then follow this with a question and answer session for ten minutes. This gives each panelist a total of thirty minutes to be in charge of the session. If a panelist is very strong in one topic, such as for sale by owners or listings, have him or her talk about that particular subject.

Have light refreshments afterward so that people can mix, ask more questions, and share their feelings about what they learned. This refreshment period can be very important to you if agents from another office have attended. Buy each panel member a small token gift for taking the time to share his or her success secrets with the group and be sure to praise each member at the end of the session before adjourning. To many top-performers, this type of recognition is more valuable than money.

Seminars

There are lots and lots of seminars out there. As an owner or manager you will be constantly receiving requests from seminar salespeople to talk at your office meetings. I hate to say no, so I select a group of three senior agents to be my guest selection committee. Any time that I get a call from a seminar salesperson asking to speak at one of my meetings, I tell the caller about my committee and ask him or her to submit something in writing about the speaker and the seminar, and the committee will then make a decision. Many of these seminars are excellent and impart great skills to the agents attending while some are far too theoretical or unrealistic in what they ask the agent to do to succeed. The point is, let your committee make the decisions, with input from you.

I would like to personally endorse the Brian Buffini seminar as one that is totally realistic regarding an agent being able to do what is recommended on an ongoing basis. It is also highly effective as a client-base building tool as it is totally founded on referrals from past and current clients and people that already know and trust you. His program truly works and doesn't require superhuman efforts to succeed.

Professional Designations

Let's talk for a few minutes about you. The better trained you are, the better you'll be able to train your sales associates and the more profits your company or office will make.

I can't stress enough how effective the Certified Residential Brokerage Manager (CRB) courses and the Certified Residential Specialist (CRS) courses are to you in developing your role as an effective leader and master salesperson.

The better trained you are, the better you'll be able to train your sales associates and the more profits your company or office will make.

The CRB courses are specifically designed to enhance your abilities as a leader and manager of a real estate firm. The CRS courses are very specifically designed to put you at the pinnacle of knowledge and resources with regards to effective real estate sales in today's highly competitive environment. These professional designations are on a parallel with, and mean the same height of professional ability as, the Certified Public Accountant (CPA) designation in the accounting industry. These designations will mark you with a highly noticeable brand of excellence in the real estate community.

Now you might ask, "Why take the CRS courses if I'm going to be a non-selling manager?" The answer is simple. Just like the sales professionals that work for you, you sell time and knowledge to them. The more of this highly effective knowledge that you have to impart to them, the more successful they are likely to become.

Remember, you are above all a leader, and the fact that you have taken these courses and have succeeded like you have says to new agents loud and clear that they should do it, too. Many of your associates will follow your example and take the courses as well.

To find out more about these courses, contact your local Board of REALTORS® or contact the National Association of REALTORS® online at REALTOR.org. Then click on Education, click on Designations/Certificates, and click on REALTOR® Family Designations and Certificate Programs.

Marketing, Advertising,
and Promotion

$\mathcal{W}$e must separate marketing from advertising. Many people make the mistake of advertising, which is designed to elicit customers to call you, when they really want to market their company.

Marketing sends a message or tells a story about your company in order to make people aware of what or who you are, and what you do. Most marketing is done through display advertising, which is designed to tell a picture story with a minimal use of the printed word. Display work is also used somewhat in advertising, primarily as an attention-getter, especially with mass-mailing pieces and the Internet.

You can sometimes get free marketing by way of sending industry-specific articles or press releases to the real estate editors of your local newspapers. Be sure to double space and use at least a twelve-point font. Include a picture of yourself. . .they just might run it along with the article.

You will have very carefully set marketing and advertising budgets in the business plan that you created before you ever opened your office and you must stick to them.

Newspapers

Newspaper advertising, including any marketing pieces that you run, is one of the three biggest expenses (along with rent and salaries) that you will have.

Every advertising dollar is precious forever, not just in the beginning. You will have to do a certain amount of newspaper advertising to pacify sellers, even if all of your other advertising is drawing you lots of customers. If carefully thought out, newspaper ads will pull in a good number of calls and result in far more revenue than the cost of the ad.

You must be careful of ad deadlines, however. Your ads must be to the paper by a certain day and time each week, and too many managers that I know wait until the last minute to decide what to advertise, throw a few ads together, and fax them in to the paper. The result is that the money is wasted because there is absolutely nothing in any of the ads that would make someone want to call. This distresses the clients because they don't like how the firm is representing their home to the public, and it distresses the agents because the floor time is not as good as it would be if the ads were better written and produced inquiries.

If you are in charge of writing the ads, set an absolute time each week to sit down with no distractions and review your listings. Pick out one or more of the best "bell ringer" homes in each of three price ranges: lower, mid, and upper end. Write an ad that whets a reader's appetite to see more and asks him or her to call to find out more. Reread the ads several *Write an ad that whets a reader's appetite to see more and asks him or her to call to find out more.* times with your buyer hat on, asking yourself, "Does this ad make me curious to know more?" If not, rewrite it until it does. The result will be a wise use of the money that you use for newspaper ads and lots of good quality calls to the agents in your office.

I do not have any problem with an agent paying for and running his or her own ads as long as I have reviewed them first and they comply with state and local laws. I find that I will often rewrite an ad for someone and have him or her come back later to compliment me on how it pulled in calls. I have a hard and fast rule that *all* advertising done by the agents in the office must be approved by me first, with absolutely no exceptions. This helps make the ads more effective and maintains the office image that I have worked hard to create. I also do not let the agents put ads in and bill the office. It only causes more work tracking them down to get paid, or waiting for an escrow to close so that I can deduct the ad from their check. The agents are business people and must maintain their own account if they are going to advertise separately. If you have someone who can track this for you, then you can have each agent pay for ads in advance and use your account.

An excellent thing to remember when writing ads is the *AIDA* formula. An ad must have four parts to be effective:

Attention. There must be something interesting in the ad's header.

Interest. The next several words must be interesting enough to make the reader want to know more.

Desire. The remainder of the ad must be carefully worded to create a pleasing picture that prompts the reader to see the property or find out more about it.

Action. You must end the ad with a call to action. For example, "Call Bob Herd for more exciting details" or "Call Bob Herd for a private walk around the serene pool" could be a call to action.

Although you will get different opinions on this, I feel strongly that the price should always be in the ad. If a reader is interested in the ad, but isn't sure if the home is in his or her price range, he or she will often just skip it and go on reading. If readers have an interest and see that it is in their price range, they will almost always call.

The local papers or "throwaways" often have an excellent ability to attract calls, and they can be much less expensive than the major publications; however, the big newspapers usually have what they call zone advertising. A newspaper like the *San Francisco Examiner* covers the entire bay area, but you can advertise in their peninsula zone only for much less money. Zone advertising in these types of major newspapers is nearly always a good use of your money.

It is important to track where your property inquiries are coming from, so develop an easy-to-use form that is kept at the floor desk that each agent can use to track where and when the calls came from. Review it about every two weeks and adjust where you spend your money accordingly. Your escrow-tracking sheet should have a line on it that asks for the client source as well and should be filled out prior to the disbursement of any commission checks. Tracking your newspaper ad effectiveness is that critical.

Mass Mailings

By the time that I started my company I was completely convinced that the way to control a major market share of a certain city or territory was with steady direct mailing to a target market, coupled with very professional prospecting. I changed my advertising budget and reduced the amount of money that I had allowed for newspaper advertising and put that money aside to reimburse my agents for part of their direct mail expenses. This worked incredibly well. I only ran a small spot ad in the newspaper on a daily basis. The bulk of my advertising went to reimburse the agents for farming materials and mass-mailing expenses.

With mass mailings you have to consider both timing and content. I found that in the Daly City market, and in several other markets that I have worked since, a well-done monthly mailing gets the best results. It is the consistency that ultimately wins the customer's business, and a monthly mailing seems to be the most effective timing to build and maintain consumer awareness of what you and your company are all about. When customers decide to use a real estate professional's services, they will contact the one that they know and feel comfortable with. This often happens even though they have never met you. After several months of mass mailing, it is not uncommon to receive a call where the caller says, "You don't know me, but we've been getting your mail and we would like you to do an appraisal on our house."

With mass mailings you have to consider both timing and content.

What you say is every bit as important as how often you say it. Consumers are not at all impressed with the fact that we are the number one office or person in the area. Why? Because none of that spells out a benefit to them, and people are only interested in what benefits them.

Every consumer has the same favorite radio station: WIIFM, or "What's In It For Me?" Every single bit of your advertising must contain a benefit to consumers or it will not stir them to call you. Most real estate companies and agents waste far too many of their advertising dollars talking about features like "I'm your neighborhood specialist," or "We are number one in your city," and so on. Every one of these overused phrases is a feature that, unless it has a benefit tied to it, means nothing and is wasted on the consumer.

A mailing that says, "In order to provide you with the cutting edge in real estate knowledge and negotiating power, I have obtained the following professional designations:" (Then spell them out). In addition, "I am the number one agent in the north peninsula because I sell my listings faster and for more money than anyone else in the area" sells a benefit and will attract a consumer's attention because he or she will potentially benefit from it. The phrase "I'm your neighborhood specialist because having an intimate knowledge of your neighborhood allows me to more effectively help people get comfortable with a decision to buy there and gets your home sold faster and at a better price" gives the consumer a clear-cut reason to call you.

Every mass mailing that you do should ask consumers to contact you, give them a reason to do so, and should have a return mailer that they can fill out and send you. In today's world the mailing should always have a way to contact you by E-mail as well.

As the owner or manager of a company, any general mass mailing that you pay for should have a company-oriented E-mail address and it should be checked at least twice daily. You can then assign any leads to the agents and reap the referral fees as an additional source of revenue.

The Internet

This ever-growing phenomenon is as much a part of a real estate brokerage firm today as the telephone. If your company doesn't have a Web page, get one. There simply isn't any other statement to be made. Your Web page will be the first interaction that many, many potential customers will have with your firm, so don't cut corners.

If your company doesn't have a web page, get one.

An effective Website offers information about the company, each agent, and the community. It should be attractive, interesting, and easy to maneuver around in. With a click of the mouse, a consumer should be able to go from the company's main page to either a branch office; directly to an agent's personal page and to that agent's personal listings or the MLS listings; or to a page that gives a short history of the community and features such as schools, churches, restaurants, and so on. Ease of use and good information capture and retain customers. Remember everyone's favorite radio station, WIIFM!

One of the best buys available today is realtor.com. (Please note that this is the *only* time that you will see the trademarked name REALTOR® in lower case). It seems that nearly every issue of REALTOR® magazine has exponentially higher numbers of "hits" on the realtor.com Website. It is simply good business to use it, since it

One of the best buys available today is realtor.com.

economically drives more and more business to you. In most cases it can be easily linked with your company's Website as well, thereby multiplying your exposure to the vast number of home buyers and sellers looking for a real estate professional to do business with.

You will need to research how much it will cost to both set up and maintain your Internet site and include those figures in your operating budget. Shop around and ask for referrals for someone that is really creative, yet cost effective. This is an important and ever-growing part of your business, so spend wisely.

Chambers of Commerce

Every Chamber of Commerce receives inquiries from individuals as well as businesses that are thinking about relocating to their area. If you are a subscribing member, they will forward these leads to you and you can make direct contact with the people that made the inquiry. This can be a good source of leads; however, you must remember that these people will be contacted by at least several other chamber members, so if you are going to attract the customer you will need to develop a relocation package that goes well beyond what the average real estate office will send.

Some firms offer cash rebates of various sorts, such as commission rebates, complimentary home protection plans and/or termite reports, and so on. This is appealing to some people and doesn't mean much to others; however, many relocation packages do not fully address the main thing on the consumer's mind, which is "I'm going to uproot my family and go to a place that I know little or nothing about, and how will my family and I cope with it all?"

The manager that carefully thinks through what every transferring family goes through, and produces brochures, news articles, and good, viable, useful information about the entire community, including real estate issues and information, will get the lion's share of these highly motivated customers.

Regular Mailings to Other Professionals

Other professionals such as doctors, attorneys, Certified Public Accountants, insurance brokers, do-it-yourself moving companies like U-Haul, managers of mini-storage facilities, and so on are an excellent target market for a mass-mailing campaign for three reasons. They buy real estate (many of those previously mentioned buy upscale and investment real estate), their clientele buy real estate and they are likely to refer them to a firm that they are familiar with, and their clientele usually have to wait awhile in their offices to be seen and are very likely to pick up and read a well-done real estate brochure or magazine that you have sent.

My experience as a sales agent and as a manager have proven that once you establish a good track record with other professionals, they are highly likely to refer you to other people that they know and do business with. You can expect this to take many months to a few years to develop, but when it happens you will reap excellent benefits.

Your first mailing should be a letter explaining who you are, if they don't already know your firm. It should state that your firm has an excellent reputation for helping professionals like them to buy or sell real estate in an efficient, orderly, and profitable manner, that you would be very interested in developing a working relationship with them, that you will be sending real estate information and brochures on a regular basis for them and their customers to review, and that you hope that they will give your firm the chance to show just how good you really are. Most mailings after that should be attractive brochures for them to give to their customers or to leave in their waiting rooms. A personal follow-up letter from you, as the broker or manager, every six months is a very, very good idea.

All mailings that you send out should have a generic telephone number and e-mail address that go to you as the manager. You can then give out the leads to the appropriate people on your sales staff and receive the referral fees back to the company. Be very careful about the placement of these referrals. Only high-quality, experienced agents should be eligible to receive these types of referrals.

Top 100 Mailing List

A highly effective thing that you, as a manager, can do for your company or office is to develop a list of the top 100 agents in your marketing area and send them regular monthly mailings of your best listings. The agents unanimously think that this is an excellent marketing and sales tool as well as a highly effective listing tool. It is also a highly effective recruiting tool.

The top 100 performers in the area will disregard your mailing as junk mail unless you carefully set it up the right way, so take the time to do it right. First, use every available resource at your disposal to identify the top 100 agents in your area. This can include MLS data, an agent advisory group from your existing company, your own knowledge of the agents in the area, and referrals or comments from professionals in other fields. Send each of them a personal letter from you explaining what you are doing, that they have been identified as one of the top 100 agents in the area, and as a result will be receiving a monthly mailing of your office's best available listings for them to show. You must make a point of the fact that every one of these properties has been pre-screened by a select committee of your best agents for effective pricing prior to inclusion in the mailing.

What worked best for me was to have submissions of listings to the committee by the seventh of the month for evaluation by the tenth and inclusion in the mailing on the fifteenth of each month. I made it clear that there were absolutely no deviations from these dates and that the agents would be responsible for creating their submissions at their own expense.

The Advantages of This Type of Mailing Are:

- You select an agent advisory committee to pre-screen the listings. This gives you a chance to recognize some agents for their seniority and/or prowess.

- Every agent will want his or her listings included in the mailing and, if rejected because of inappropriate pricing, it is an excellent tool for agents to use to get a price adjustment.

- The top 100 agents selected by you are quite flattered to have been selected and your relationship with them goes to a new level. This is an excellent recruiting tool and gives you a very focused group from which to recruit from.

- This is a powerful listing tool.

- This increases showings and sales of your inventory, increasing bottom line profit due to less marketing time and expenses.

- You get the reputation of being a very "cutting-edge," innovative office manager.

Brochures

Go and talk to several "quick print" types of printing companies. Tell them that your company or office will be making a large number of brochures every month, probably in the thousands very soon, and you are getting bids for the work. Have them show you samples of expensive, mid-range, and inexpensive property brochures and flyers that they have done for other companies and give you a price list for a guarantee of one thousand, three thousand, five thousand, seven thousand, and ten thousand per month. Be sure that they know that you are getting competitive bids so that they give you their best price.

Let your agents know what you have negotiated for their benefit and at the same time let them know that using the copy machine as a printing press will not be tolerated. Explain to them that you do not want copy-machine quality brochures going out to the public as this is below the standard that you have set for the office. Be honest and tell them that it is not in your operating budget to support this type of use of the copy machines.

Set a certain standard of quality for your top 100 mailings and let the sales staff know that anything submitted below that standard will be rejected. Include the brochures in your mailings to other professionals. Keep and maintain a display area for the brochures in the lobby of your office for people to take as they come in and out of your office. Instruct someone on your administrative staff to check it and refill it every day in the morning.

Office Meetings

Office meetings are the most effective means available to give information in a timely manner. Meetings also build the office culture by getting a large number of the agents to interact with each other, provide a forum for new listing and sales information, provide agent recognition, and give updates on new and recurring legal and operational issues.

> *Office meetings are the most effective means available to give information in a timely manner.*

Your office meetings must be interesting to attend or you will get a low turnout and they will not be effective. They should probably not exceed forty-five minutes to an hour at the very longest, and guest speakers should be limited to once a month and not more than ten minutes in duration. I have a folder that I put items in all week and an "office meeting notes" file in my word processor that I use to elaborate on what I want to say at each meeting.

I start preparing for my next meeting as soon as the current one is finished. I am constantly looking for items that are worthy of being on the agenda. As I find them, I file them in the office-meeting file or make notes about them in my computer file. Sometimes I just jot a few words on a piece of paper and put it in the file to remind me of an agenda item.

Start on Time, Every Time

All agents view their time as precious, and nothing irritates them more than waiting around for a meeting to start because the same people show up late every week.

Out of respect for the agents that do show on time, I start the meeting exactly on time at 9:00 A.M. If people straggle in late we just ignore them. If they insist on disrupting the group by walking in and turning everyone's attention, then I just stare quietly at them until they either leave or look at me. Then I just stare at them a little longer in that "certain way." It's very effective.

Written Agenda

I find that I get the best attendance if I post a written office meeting agenda on the bulletin board and e-mail a copy to every agent two days before the meeting. My meetings always start promptly at 9:00 A.M. and finish at or before 10:00 A.M. Those that come in late simply miss part. I make a point of saying that I value their time and will not hold them up for latecomers.

I always start with the introduction of new agents. Next, my in-house loan representative quotes the current interest rates to the group and often gives a brief summary of why they have moved up or down, as the case may be. This also gets the sales agents familiar with him and gets them to use him more. Next is the guest speaker, if any. Then I will do something relating to agent recognition: Quote a legal issue, usually from the Association bulletin; state agent birthdays and anniversaries with the company; talk about any problems that have arisen, ask if anyone has something for the group to hear, then ask for agents with new listings or price changes to come up and talk about them. I will also list as an agenda item such things as recruiting, when I need their help with names; any special listings or sales made or company records broken; and things of that nature.

Motivational Quote

At the bottom of my office meeting agenda, I always insert a motivational quote. I have gotten wonderful feedback from my agents about this over the years. I am always looking for them. One of the best sources is a book by Anthony Robbins, *Unlimited Power;* however, I also get them from my TOP PRODUCER program, *Reader's Digest,* and so on. Be creative! Real estate sales can be a challenging job, and a motivational quote from a world-class person like Earl Nightingale or Anthony Robbins can really help sometimes.

Guest Speaker

Guest speakers can be an excellent way to bring timely information to your agents and are certainly a relevant and necessary part of some office meetings. The termite inspector that brings in a termite-eaten or dry-rotted board to show the agents what they look like is fun and informative. The title or escrow company sales representative or lender that wants to come in and "just say hello" is all right about once every six months or so, and the memory-training expert and other "gurus" that are simply looking for a captive audience really should be avoided.

There is nothing that will drive your agents away from office meetings as fast as a constant array of speakers that are, for the most part, irrelevant to the agents' listing and selling activities. Speakers that ignore your ten-minute limit and drone on and on until you cut them off (and you must cut them off) are the worst. If they violate your ten-minute rule, put them on a list and do not let them come back. Tell your agents that you have done this and they will really appreciate it.

> *There is nothing that will drive your agents away from office meetings as fast as a constant array of speakers that are, for the most part, irrelevant to the agents' listing and selling activities.*

You need to maintain a good relationship with title companies and most lenders and other direct support industries. The best way to diplomatically pick and choose the correct ones while avoiding the overbearing and inappropriate ones is to form a speaker review committee with three of your senior agents.

If someone who you are interested in approaches you about being a speaker, make an appointment. If you aren't entirely sure, state that you have a speaker review committee that decides who the speakers are. Encourage the speaker to submit something in writing that you can bring up at the next committee meeting. Even if you don't actually have such a committee, this can nonetheless be an effective way of handling the situation.

Tour of Office Listings

A weekly tour of your new office listings has many benefits: It gets the agents physically to each house, which pleases both the sellers and the listing agents; it makes floor time more productive as most of the floor time agents have actually seen the property that callers are inquiring about and are therefore better prepared to answer questions about it, which will very often lead to more appointments; and it gets the agents to interact while touring together and come to know each other better, forming a tighter bond between them.

I have the greater metro area where I work broken down into three areas. We tour up to eight homes in each one on a rotational basis. My office meetings and the property tour are every Tuesday right after the office meeting and any agent wanting a home on tour that Tuesday must turn in a written request to my listing administrator along with a copy of the MLS listing printout by 3 P.M. on Friday.·

My listing administrator makes up around ten "tour packages" late Monday afternoon. Each package includes a city map with the properties numbered in an orderly fashion to allow minimal driving, the MLS printout of each property in its proper order on the tour, and two critique sheets with spots for four properties each on them. They are available in the reception area right after the meeting and the agents are asked to take only one per car.

The forms allow the agents, as a group, to rate each home as to its effective pricing and condition as well as providing a place for comments and constructive criticism. These are given back to the listing administrator after the tour, who gives all of the critique sheets to each listing agent to share with the sellers.

Floor Schedule Sign-Up

Our company currently controls over 40 percent of the listings in our metro area and our floor time is very productive. With over 140 agents in my office, you can imagine the demand for floor time. Actually, a lot of the experienced agents don't take it as they are working completely by referral, but the competition is still strong.

At the end of the second office meeting of each month, my receptionist puts the calendar for the next month's floor time out on her counter area. Each agent signs up for a maximum of three times per month on a first come, first served basis. The calendar is left out for three days or until filled completely. If not filled completely by then, which rarely happens, I go to some of the new agents and "recommend" that they take some floor time.

This creates a competitive demand for floor time and gets agents to sign up for it with a minimal amount of work on the part of the administrative staff.

Agent Recognition/Annual Awards

There is little else that you can do as a manager to retain and motivate your sales staff that is as effective as recognizing them for their efforts. This should be sincere and should be done on a regular basis.

As the broker or manager, it will be your responsibility to review and initial each listing and sales contract that goes through your office. I try to save contract review for early mornings or late afternoons when there are fewer distractions in

There is little else that you can do as a manager to retain and motivate your sales staff that is as effective as recognizing them for their efforts.

the office. After I sign off on all of the current files, I call the voice mail of each agent that brought one in and leave a short message congratulating him or her on the new listing or sale and I tell each how much I appreciate all of the hard work. It's short, simple, and cost effective, and the agents love it.

Some offices have perpetual trophies or plaques that the top listing agent and top selling agent get each month. I don't use these because too often they go to the same three or four people in the office. The rest then stop trying for them after a time and they tend to lose their meaning. This method will probably work well in a start-up office, however, or one in which the agents are fairly evenly balanced and there aren't any superstars.

I like to take my "better" agents out to lunch from time to time. It's a nice way to say thanks and it also gives me a chance to ask about the pulse of the office from their perspective. They all know that I'm open to constructive criticism as well as compliments and they will always bring me up-to-date on any gossip, rumors, who's being recruited by another firm and so on. I get huge mileage from this and I always end the lunch by telling them how much I appreciate the work that they do.

My company has a questionnaire that we send out to every client and customer after we close each escrow that asks how we did as a company, how our agent did, where we can improve, what made them select us to do business with, and it rates our agent from 1 to 10. I get a large number of these back each month and I read them at the office meetings. It's great agent recognition, often humorous, and makes the meeting more fun.

At least five or more times a day I get out of my office and just walk around the office. Whenever I get the chance to stop an agent in front of someone else and give him or her a sincere compliment about something, such as a new listing, sale, how he or she handled a situation, and so on, I do it. It too

At least five or more times a day I get out of my office and just walk around the office.

pays big dividends. More on Management By Walking Around (MBWA) will be covered in the next chapter.

A company picnic, holiday party, volleyball tournament, or annual "kickoff" breakfast are all excellent times to give out the annual agent recognition awards. I give out first, second, and third place awards for top listing agent and top selling agent in two categories, volume and number of transactions. This rewards both the luxury home agents and the starter home agents. I also give trophies for the most inbound referrals sold and the most outbound referrals sent, a Rookie of The Year award, and, finally, a Top-Performer award. These sixteen awards make the ceremony just the right length and is within my budget. Sometimes I will give out a "Worst Client of the Year" award as well, which always ends the ceremony on a fun note.

Each month my company posts the "Top 100" statistics and the "Listing Ladder" statistics. Each time I put them up I make sure to get around the office and ask a few people if they have seen the new Top 100 and Listing Ladder lists that I posted. Before you know it, word has spread and there are people dropping by all day to check things out. Someone is always excited to see that he or she has moved up or onto the Top 100 list or made the Listing Ladder. It's great public recognition and creates just the right amount of peer pressure for non-performance. My office always has eighteen to twenty-five agents on the Top 100 list and I call every one of them and tell them how proud I am of them and congratulate them for their efforts.

The Listing Ladder is a posting of each agent and how many listings he or she has taken year to date, in descending order. The list is separated into two categories. It takes twelve listings a year to be a member of the Listing Society, so these members are posted first as the list is in descending order, then the Listing Club is posted just under that as a separate category. We have quarterly patio parties for everyone who is on track to be a member of the Listing Society. As an example, we have a party in mid-April for each person that had three or more listings at the end of March, one in mid-July for everyone who had six listings by the end of June, and so on. We also have a plaque in a prominent place in the office where each member's name is placed as soon as he or she reaches twelve listings.

Day-To-Day Operations

$\mathcal{S}$et a minimum standard and enforce it. This is probably one of the most important things that you can learn from this entire book! You and your company or office will be judged by your lowest producer. That is so important that I'll repeat

Set a minimum standard and enforce it.

it. You and your company or office will be judged by your lowest producer.

As a part of your initial planning, you must decide what type of an office or firm you are going to have. What are you willing to accept as your "minimum standard" of production and conduct?

As far as conduct goes, anything less than top of the line is not acceptable. People with bad reputations should be avoided, no matter what their production is or has been. If they inquire, be tactful, but let them down gently. Once you hire someone with a known bad "track record," it will ruin your chances of hiring many other good agents since they will not want to work with that individual. If you are interviewing a new agent or an experienced agent that you really don't know, you must ask for references or past clients to call and ask questions of. All agents get a "rep" and are pretty easy to check out locally after awhile. Hiring an unethical agent, or one with a less-than-desirable personality, says to the world that you are willing to tolerate bad or unethical behavior and/or low production. Don't allow it from the start.

If you do make a mistake in hiring, as I have done every now and then, try for a short but reasonable time to correct it. Call the agents in, tell them right out what is and is not acceptable, and that you will not tolerate any more of the offending behavior, then enforce your statements. Any blatant unethical conduct should never be tolerated and the offender should be immediately terminated. You will be absolutely amazed at how positively your dismissal actions will be received by the rest of your sales and administrative staff. I fired my second-highest producer on the spot for taking another agent's clients. His production was missed, but only for a short time. As word of his firing spread and other experienced agents liked what they heard, they decided to work with me very soon thereafter.

Setting a minimum production standard is fairly simple. You simply take the total cost to run your office for the entire year, add a reasonable profit (this can vary from 2 percent to approximately 11 percent, depending on your market), and that is your "desk cost," which becomes your minimum standard. As a part of your hiring process, each agent should be charged with meeting or exceeding your minimum standard and told that no one is allowed to work for your office or company unless he or she meets or exceeds the minimum standard. If you make it clear right up front, your agents should always exceed it. Those that can't for some reason will almost always fire themselves. The critically important thing in the equation is you. You must enforce the minimum standard uniformly or your operation will suffer financially.

I find that a monthly assessment of each agent helps to spot trends early on. In contrast, a quarterly review with at-risk agents that are below your minimum standard shows them that you care and will help them, but that you will still hold them accountable. This type of help and accountability will either make them become productive or leave, usually in fairly short order.

I find that a monthly assessment of each agent helps to spot trends early on.

I make it a habit to let new or transfer agents know that they are expected to be on track with quarterly minimum standard earnings by the end of the third quarter after they are hired. Because I make them accountable, they do it. I almost never have to let someone go for low production.

Agent Dispute Resolution

There are two types of agent disputes that can arise: a dispute with you and/or your office policies, and a dispute with another agent in your office. An agent that has some sort of problem with you, the company, or another agent, and allows the problem to continue, can create an enormous distraction and get other agents involved, which can generally create havoc in the office. These issues, once identified, must be settled as fairly as possible as soon as possible, with no exceptions.

If your agents have a dispute with you, ask them to sit down with you and clearly outline what is bothering them. If they are reluctant to do this, ask them to put it in a letter to you that you can read, then meet with them. When you do meet with them, give them your full attention, with no phone calls or interruptions. Hear them out fully, then, if you feel it is appropriate, answer their questions and address their problem. If you need time to assess a company policy or look into a matter first, set a time to get back with them to resolve the issue if it can be resolved. If their frustration with you or the office is in direct conflict with what you believe to be good operational policies, such as how referrals are given out or something of that nature, then you will simply need to state why you need to keep things as they are as clearly as possible and maintain control of your office. If it's a big enough issue with them after it has been explained, they may leave, but if you start making separate deals with each agent that has a problem with the way that you run your operation you will soon be so fragmented that you will have lost complete control of the office, and the agents will be running it instead of you.

If two or more of the agents in your office have an issue with one another, you should have an agent dispute committee available in your office or company to handle these matters. If the problem is covered under a company policy then it probably falls on you, as the manager, to call the parties together, restate the company policy, ask for any questions, answer them, and put an end to it.

If other issues arise that need an impartial hearing, then a panel of three or five agents, plus you as moderator, should be assembled. Each agent to the dispute should be able to select one or two panel members, and the disputees should jointly select the last one. This way you get as impartial a hearing as possible. As soon after the dispute arises as possible, set a time for the hearing. Each side should be able to present its case, then each side should be allowed a short rebuttal time. After that, the parties should be dismissed and the panel should evaluate the matter and make a decision that the parties have already agreed as being final and binding. By the way, being on this panel is an excellent way of recognizing some of your agents.

Praise in Public, Criticize in Private

Anyone who has been in real estate for even a short time knows that there are plenty of crazy, off-the-wall things that can happen on a daily basis. The way that agents handle these situations can be the source of everything from extreme delight at a job very well done, to sheer anger at a situation bungled beyond repair.

When an agent does something that is commendable, be sure to make the most of it and praise him or her publicly. It makes agents feel wonderful and glad that they are a part of your team and ready to go out and do it again. Other people that hear your praise will want to emulate the behavior that initiated it and will like you for giving it to the agents that deserve it.

> *When an agent does something that is commendable, be sure to make the most of it and praise him or her publicly.*

When agents do something that is negative in some way, it is time for them to hear about it from you immediately! However, you will get far better results by "requesting" that they see you in your office than you will by embarrassing them in front of other people (this includes your administrative staff). Call them into your office when you are prepared. Close the door and ask them if they know why you called them in. This will often invoke a self-criticism that you will have to do little else about. If they are unsure of what they have done, tell them directly and clearly what the violation was. Ask them if they understand the consequences of their actions. Ask for their input if you deem it appropriate. Once you have their input and their clarity on why you and others consider it a violation, either ask them what they are willing to do about it or tell them what corrective action you expect to see take place. Let them know that you will not tolerate any further issues of that sort and that you will be monitoring the issue or situation.

Everyone has a degree of pride and self-esteem; therefore, a public dressing-down is almost never appropriate. Your handling of the issue in a private and constructive way will be both appreciated and constructive in all but the most rare instances.

If one of your agents does something that is clearly grounds for dismissal, call that person into your office, explain the situation and why you consider it grounds for dismissal, then state that he or she is terminated, effective immediately. If you do this, stand your ground without getting into an argument. If you are going to terminate someone, just do it.

I fired my second-best performer on the spot in 1976. A referral buyer called my office on a Saturday for one of my agents. This person took the call and said that the agent wasn't available but he could help him. He took the person out, sold him a home by Sunday, and opened the escrow on Monday. On Wednesday, the other agent came in to see me, very angry. He told me that a friend of his had just called and said, "Well, I guess you owe me a referral fee." When asked, his friend explained that the buyer had called him to tell him that he had bought a house from my office. I called the first agent into my office and asked him to explain himself. He admitted that he had sold the person a house and figured that no one would really know. I fired him on the spot!

While I wasn't happy about losing his production, I was incensed at his lack of ethics. The rest of the people in the office applauded my actions and, overall, it helped me to recruit even more agents. That sort of news travels fast in the real estate community, and people knew that they could work for me and not be subjected to misbehavior by other people.

The same rule of praise in public, criticize in private applies to your administrative staff as well. It only takes one administrative person with a bad attitude to upset your entire sales staff and even cause some of them to leave.

If you encounter attitude problems, tardiness, too much sick time off, or any other type of less-than-satisfactory behavior, you must address it in private with the offenders, and right away. If they are habitually late, leave early, or take too long a lunch, tell them that this is not tolerable and that you will be monitoring the situation from now on.

If they are employees and not independent contractors, your chances of getting a wrongful termination suit filed against you are increased, so you must be careful to document your case very carefully by keeping a log of when they arrive and leave, how often they fail to show up for work, and so on. After you have built a case that you feel supports your position, call them in, tell them that you have been monitoring the situation, that it hasn't improved, and that you are terminating them, effective immediately. Ask for their keys and other company belongings, ask them to clean out their desk, and state you will send them a check for what is due them the following day.

I need to qualify the previous paragraph by saying that it is advice given to me by our company's attorney. You should absolutely contact your own legal counsel for advice in these matters as employee/employer rights issues may vary from state to state.

Handling the High-Producing Troublemaker

Hiring or developing a high-producing agent is probably one of the most rewarding things that you can do as a manager; however, every now and then you will make a mistake and hire a high producer that isn't compatible with you and your operation, or a salesperson that you have developed into a high producer will let his or her ego get the best of him or her.

When either of these things happen you can find yourself on the receiving end of someone who is constantly complaining or making unjust remarks about you and your office or company.

If you allow this type of person to continue his or her criticism unabated, it *will* begin to affect the rest of your sales staff. The tension will mount unabated until you have a crisis on your hands that could even include a mass walkout by your sales staff.

When this type of situation starts (and believe me, it happens to all of us) you have to tackle the matter head on and early. The best way is to ask the individuals to meet with you privately. Let them know that you've been hearing that they are unhappy about some things and that you feel that it's best to put things out on the table where they can be looked over carefully and addressed, if necessary.

Have your own agenda of things that you have either heard they have said or are upset about. Start the meeting by telling them that you value them very much as an important part of your team, but that you have heard that they are unhappy about a few things and you wanted to talk with them about those specific issues and any other things that they would like to bring up. Then go immediately into your agenda, which is what you have heard or observed. Address each issue individually by first stating what it is and then ask them for their input on it. Keep good notes so that you can analyze them after the meeting and decide on a course of action.

Sometimes a person just needs to vent, sometimes there are legitimate concerns about the way that things are done in your office or company, and sometimes people are too "me-oriented" to see why their concerns are not for the good of the entire group. Often it will be a combination of all three and that is why it is important to take notes. It can actually be a growth experience for you.

If it turns out that most, if not all, of their concerns are petty gripes or unreasonable demands, you need to say so and explain why. It is very important that you also tell the individuals in a very straightforward manner that their activities are a disruption to the rest of the sales staff and that they will have to end if they wish to continue to work there. To end the meeting, tell them again how much you appreciate all of their efforts on your behalf, acknowledge anything that you agree should be changed, and remind them of activities that they must curtail. Thank them for the meeting.

It is critical that you make any adjustments or changes that you said you would do. It is also critical that you monitor the agents' activities as well. If you continue to see the offensive or unacceptable behavior, then you must call them in and tell them that, although you have made the changes agreed to, they haven't, and that you feel it is best for them to move on to another company. Believe it or not, just doing this will often be enough for them to take you seriously, ask for another chance, and stop the activity. However, if you ask them to leave, you must be prepared to back it up. If you do agree to another chance, be adamant that it is your office or company and that you feel that your policies are fair and will not be changed. They either need to accept this or move on; no more trouble will be tolerated.

It is critical that you make any adjustments or changes that you said you would do.

I once hired a fellow that I used to work with before I became a real estate professional. He was promoted to a low-level management position before I was and somehow felt that this should carry over into our new lives as real estate agents. He was, unbeknownst to me, very jealous of my success and the success of my company. He started spreading some very vicious rumors about me to the rest of the sales staff. After being off for six weeks with a bad back injury, I could sense that something was wrong when I returned. It was too late. I had not put a stop to it in time and he had incited my ten best agents to leave and open their own company. It took me almost one year of very hard work to rebuild the company to the same level as before.

Get Out of Your Office or Management By Walking Around (MBWA)

Almost every broker/owner or manager has a private office. It comes with the territory. It can, however, also serve to separate you from the "goings-on" in the office and make you seem reserved or too remote to many of your sales agents.

We managers are all extremely busy reviewing contracts, reading up on new legislation or laws, making and returning calls, interviewing potential new agents, and so on. However, I have found that it is quite important to leave my door open and make a point of telling people that they may come in at any time that I'm not on the phone or with someone. It is very important that you are easily accessible.

I make it a point to get out of my office and just walk around about five times a day. I currently manage a 16,000 square foot building with over 140 agents, so I go in different directions each time. This is better for my health than sitting all day and it also gives me a chance to get out among the agents where I have a chance to talk informally with them one-on-one or in small groups. It is also a chance to praise someone for that new sale or listing, for obtaining his or her brokers license, or positive things of that nature. It also gives me a chance to hear much more of the local gossip, both in and out of the office, which allows me to be better prepared to deal with many situations. I constantly get little tidbits from agents and staff alike about who's unhappy at another office or who's upset with our computers and many other "heads up" kind of things that help me to stay ahead of the competition and keep my agents happy. Awareness is critical in this business and you just can't get enough information sitting in your office all day.

Awareness is critical in this business and you just can't get enough information sitting in your office all day.

Administrative and Sales Staff Reviews

Human nature being what it is, everyone likes to know if they are performing up to a reasonable standard. The only way that this can happen is for you, as the manager, to set reasonable, well-thought-out standards, enforce them, and provide periodic opportunities to tell those that you manage how they are doing. Staff reviews are the most efficient way to do this.

I have administrative staff meetings, which are group meetings, once or twice a month. I open the meeting by going over my agenda. We pretty much keep this meeting to general operational matters such as supplies, escrows and listings, advertising deadlines, any problems that they are encountering with other people, and things of that nature. However, if one of the staff has performed exceptionally well at something I always take the time to recognize him or her for it in front of the others. I also recognize their birthdays and anniversaries with the company. I normally see them individually about any negative issues unless they all need to hear about it.

Each November I hold an annual meeting with each employee to help set the goals and commitments for the following year. It is crucial that the agent set up his or her goals, not you, although you can certainly give input. You should carefully determine what excites each employee you meet with. For example, an employee excited about being in the top five in the company will not be overly enthused about setting a goal based on volume sales. Likewise, an agent who wants thirty escrows next year won't be as interested in a goal focusing on doing $6,000,000 worth of business. You need to offer several different ways to measure success and see which one or ones excite each individual employee. This is also a good time to bring up the minimum production standard, if appropriate. Naturally, someone who is consistently well above it won't need the reminder, but someone performing near or below it could use a refresher.

In addition, determine the rewards that will come once the goals are achieved. For example, the agent may buy a laptop computer after reaching the four-month goal, $1,500 worth of new clothes after achieving the eight-month goal, and a new car or vacation upon reaching the annual goal. It's a good idea to encourage each agent to get pictures of the rewards, placed where they can be seen, to serve as an additional motivator.

I review each agent's listing and sales production and meet with each as needed, usually every three to four months, to discuss how things are going. I seldom schedule a formal meeting with the good producers as I openly compliment them all along the way anyway, but agents that are working near or below the annualized minimum standard get called in at least every three months. I let them know that this is a review of their production for the last quarter and I ask them to have ideas ready for me that they think will benefit their production.

When we meet, the first thing that I do is to tell them that I am concerned about their production and I want to explore what we can both do to help them to get it where it belongs. The worse their production, the worse they hate these meetings. It is not uncommon for low-producing agents to fire themselves prior to these types of meetings.

On occasion you will have a good agent that will hit a slump. This can be the result of anything from burnout to a divorce. When this happens, and you see their production fall off, be especially supportive. Tell them that you understand what they are going through and that you know that they are strong enough to get through it and to just stay focused. Ask if there is anything that you can do to make it easier for them. These meetings are also excellent opportunities to ask them for the name of an agent at another company that they would like to see working at your company.

Policies and Procedures Manual

This is your office or company and you are the person responsible for setting the parameters by which it is run; however, due to the very independent and diverse nature of what makes a good real estate agent, it can be frustrating for agents to work for a company that does not have a clear set of guidelines under which to operate. For instance, the last company that an agent worked at may have had an entirely different philosophy about how to handle the presentation of multiple counteroffers than you do. If you do not have things of this nature spelled out clearly, you can't expect your sales agents to abide by your wishes.

I won't go into philosophical differences here about the many and varied things that should be addressed in a policies and procedures manual. There are many good "boiler plate" examples available today from the educational divisions of the National Association of REALTORS® and many state associations. I urge you to get one during the very first part of your new office planning, read it thoroughly several times, then add or embellish on anything that you feel needs to be more particularly addressed in your version.

Among the items to consider are payment of commissions; company commission schedule; commission notes; reduced agent commission if he or she has left the company; taking reduced commission listings; floor time: who, when, hours, days of coverage; vacation coverage; release of listings if one leaves the company; dispute resolution; office meetings; company-paid reimbursement program for professional designations; selling commercial real estate, including business opportunities, land, and subdivision sales; listing and selling "out of area" properties; what to say and do if faced with litigation or a "demand letter;" advertising policy: where, when, who pays?; use of office machines; number of mailings allowed each day/week; what duties the support staff will perform for the agents, and when; request to use in-house lender or title company; and agent sale or purchase of own property.

Sign the Voluntary Affirmative Marketing Agreement (VAMA)

Discrimination is absolutely intolerable and should be avoided at all costs. Signing the VAMA says to the world that you truly believe that and agree to conduct yourself and your company in harmony with such beliefs. It is simply the right way to do business!

Do the Most Unpleasant Tasks First Every Day

If you have ever had the need to confront an unpleasant person or must let someone down for any reason, you know how easy it is to procrastinate and avoid it. I have found over the years that procrastination and avoidance don't make the problems or situations go away, they only serve to ruin the better part of your day until you finally take them on and dispose of them.

Once this became obvious to me, I decided that every time I had an unpleasant task to perform, I would do it as soon as possible each day. It wasn't long until I noticed that my productivity had gone up and life in general seemed to get a little better. All I really did was to tackle the inevitable early on and give myself the rest of the day to perform at a higher and better level. It really does work, so try it.

Maintain Control, No Matter What the Cost

After opening or taking over your office, you will be hiring more and more agents and support personnel. The more people that you hire, the more divergent your group will be. You will seldom make decisions that will make everyone happy, so be sure to analyze each decision carefully to be sure that it is as sound and reasonable as possible for the good of the entire group. The crucial thing is to *make* a decision. Issues left unresolved seldom go away, and have a way of accumulating and building frustration amongst your agents. I have even seen this escalate into a mass walkout in some real estate offices.

In doing this you will sometimes encounter an individual, or group of individuals, that disagree with your decisions. If you know that your decisions are founded on good judgment, stand your ground and do not give in to special interest groups or factions within your office. To do so is to say to your entire office that you are a weak leader and that you can be intimidated into making decisions that favor a faction in your office instead of sticking with decisions that you know are best for everyone in the office. Remember, to be an effective leader, you do not necessarily need to be liked by everyone, but it is crucial that everyone respects you or they will not continue to work for you.

> *Remember, to be an effective leader, you do not necessarily need to be liked by everyone, but it is crucial that everyone respects you or they will not continue to work for you.*

A decision that is as fair as possible for the entire group, and that is well explained, will almost never create any lasting controversy. Just remember that being clear to the group about what you have done and why gives them the feeling that they were important enough to you and your organization that you felt a need to "keep them in the loop."

I once had a sales agent that, after he got his brokers license, suddenly felt that he knew a lot more than I did. He started openly questioning nearly every decision that I made, including getting small groups of agents together behind my back to "discuss" many of my decisions. It didn't take more than a couple of weeks for me to get my fill of his "new found" knowledge. I called him in, confronted him with the meetings, told him that it was my company and that my decisions were for the benefit of all and if he disagreed with them to the extent that he did that he was better off transferring to another company. He didn't get the hint, and, after a couple more instances, I called him in and fired him. The mood in the office immediately changed for the better. It turns out that many of the agents that he was constantly complaining to were very uncomfortable about it, but didn't know how to tell me. The point is it's *your* company. Control it at any cost.

Stay Healthy—Take Time for Yourself

Given what I experienced, this may be the most important lesson yet. My real estate company was very profitable, making me a six-figure net income in the late seventies. I enjoyed the day-to-day issues that I encountered running it and the prestige that came with creating it. I worked very hard at it; at least six days a week, and for many hours a day.

What I didn't realize was that a severe back and neck injury that I had suffered many years before while playing football would come back to haunt me because I was so busy nurturing the business that I forgot to nurture the businessman. It was 1977 and we had moved into a beautiful home that I had just purchased. I moved many of the boxes myself and had strained my back "a little." One day a few weeks thereafter, I bent down to put my shoes on and simply fell over. I spent the next six weeks flat on my back and I have never been the same since. I was in so much pain that I simply could not keep pace with what it took to run my company, and I had no choice but to sell it.

You have to fully understand the importance of your leadership to the success of your company or office. Without you at the helm, in good physical and mental condition, your company simply will not be the same organization. It will not be as profitable and will not run as well. Managing a real estate office or company can often be physically and emotionally challenging. It is an absolute must that you take the time to exercise regularly to keep yourself physically healthy and in shape, and to take sufficient time off to stay emotionally balanced and focused so that you are up to the task.

> *You have to fully understand the importance of your leadership to the success of your company or office.*

The Golden Parachute Desk

Suppose you either own a company or have taken over a branch office that has several agents that have been good, steady producers for many years and have always remained loyal to the company. They have invested well, are financially set up, and are getting up in years now, so they really don't want to work that hard anymore. The trouble is that none of them are currently meeting your "desk cost," so what do you do? You've got to have more production out of these desks in order to stay as profitable as possible but you can't just tell these people to leave. That wouldn't be right; besides, cumulatively they are a huge asset.

I ran into this problem three times in my career. The first time that I encountered it, I sat down by myself, with a legal pad, and just began to jot down the problem on one side of the page and possible solutions on the other side.

What I came up with was what I call my Golden Parachute Desk. I met with the "retired" agents and explained to them that I was starting to feel the pinch from their cumulative lower production mode and that I needed their help in order to correct the situation. Most of them were back to 50/50 to 60/40 commission splits due to their lower production, so I explained that I valued them very much as friends, agents, and a company resource. I told them that I needed to get more production from each of the desks and that I realized that they were comfortable working at their current pace. I told them that I had created a Golden Parachute Desk for senior agents like them that had a minimum of ten years with the company and were at least sixty years old. I told them that if they would agree to share the desk with some of the other senior agents that I would put them at a 70 percent commission split permanently. I also told them that, because of their vast experience, I would appreciate it very much if they would be around the office a little to help out with questions from the junior agents as well. This made them feel needed and an integral part of the office. They were pleased with it.

As I said, I have done this three times now and I have never had a senior agent say no. The bonus is that the desk that all of them now occupy is very productive from their cumulative efforts and I have freed up three to six other desks to put younger, more productive agents in. Overall my office production increased by several million dollars a year each time.

Maintain a Reasonable Financial Reserve

This applies to your company and your personal finances. If you are managing a large real estate company, you will have little, if anything, to do with the decisions that they make about their financial reserves. If you own your own company then you are probably the only decision maker involved with this issue and you must take it seriously!

Depending on the size of your organization, it is probably a reasonable goal to ultimately have a one-year operating capital reserve account. Of course you will have to build up to this, but start just as soon as your company is operating profitably. Put as much of your net profit away each month as you can.

Anyone that has been around the real estate business for a few years can tell you that it goes through cycles. If you start your company during a boom cycle and spend all that you make, you will surely be in for an unpleasant surprise when the market changes, interest rates increase, and sales slow down. During the late eighties I was approached by several different brokers about buying their firms, but I knew that they had been taking every penny out of the company and that they were in financial trouble. Most of them closed and, not only did the broker lose his entire investment, several support people and their families were affected by the loss of a job as well.

Positioning your company with a good financial reserve can also bring many opportunities your way. For instance, when the market does slow down and other firms are financially stressed or close, it creates some tremendous recruiting and hiring opportunities for you. Since you have the financial reserve to maintain your marketing programs at or near normal operating levels, your company is a more productive place for top performers to work and many will seek you out.

A side benefit to having a healthy financial reserve is that you carry a lot of weight with your banker. Without touching it, you can turn your reserve account into lines of credit for guaranteed-sale programs, no-fee accounts, and other financial benefits.

It is equally important that you maintain a healthy personal financial reserve. If you suffer from a health issue as I did, or if the market slows and you need or want to temporarily reduce or eliminate your salary, you will have the flexibility to do so without any adverse effects on your personal finances or credit history. Maintaining a healthy financial reserve also means that you have cash available to take advantage of financial opportunities when they present themselves. Being a real estate professional, you are on the cutting edge of knowing about new property coming up for sale. When that perfect property suddenly presents itself, you want to be ready.

Take time to reflect and plan. At least annually, you should take the time to get away by yourself somewhere that is very comfortable to you and reflect back on the year that just passed. Have pen and paper handy to jot down notes as you rethink the year.

Take time to reflect and plan.

Take this same time to refine and adjust your one-year, three-year, and five-year business plans. Once done to your liking, give a copy to your regional manager or the company owner if you are a

Ask Yourself These Questions:

- What went wrong, and what could I have done differently to change the outcome?

- Who affected my life, and in what way?

- Whose life did I affect, and in what way?

- How well off are my company and I financially, and if less than desired, specifically what will I do about it?

- Has my vision for the company changed? If so, how?

- What do I want to achieve personally next year, and specifically how will I make it happen?

- What do I want the company to achieve next year, and specifically how will I make it happen?

- What will the market be like next year and what can I do to take maximum advantage of it?

branch manager, or give a copy to your CPA and banker if you are an owner. You will get amazing mileage out of this as nothing pleases a regional manager, owner, or banker as much as seeing that you have put deep thought into the future success of your office or company.

Plan for Your Retirement

Given reasonably good health, real estate office management is probably something that you can do well into your seventies if you want to. However, there is much to be said for working because you want to, and not because you have to, by your fifties or sooner. To achieve this, you must do some careful retirement planning, even though you may be fortunate enough to never retire.

I would strongly suggest that you start funding an IRA or SEP-IRA to its maximum every year. Put money away for this monthly or at least quarterly or you may often find that when the deadline comes that you don't have enough available funds. There is real magic in tax-deferred compounded interest and it can make for a very comfortable retirement all by itself if started early enough.

Buy and hold well-located real estate, even if you must start with a small condominium in a good building. Buy for location as this brings maximum rents and appreciation over time. Do not ever sell one of these properties; simply keep them, maintain them, and don't be "Mr. Good Guy." Raise your rents every time a lease expires.

What seems like a very small cash flow now will be huge by the time that you decide to retire or cut back. If you are inclined to own a large apartment complex or a piece of commercial property as a part of your retirement income then you will need to do a tax-deferred exchange every three to five years from condominium to rental home to small or medium apartment house to large apartment complex or commercial property. My favorite investments are self-storage facilities, or mini-storage facilities, as they always have an on-site manager, low operating expenses, are fairly easy to maintain, and offer substantial cash flow.

The most important issue here is to start early and discipline yourself to be constant in your retirement savings.

Selling Your Company

The reasons for selling your real estate company are varied and can include health, retirement, divorce, moving to another area, career change, a decision to go back into sales, and many others. You have many factors to consider when selling your company, but the most important one is that your company's greatest asset is the sales staff. Without them, you merely have a bunch of used furniture and office equipment to sell.

The first step is to let your CPA know that you want to sell your company and have him or her prepare your books to reflect your current financial position. Money matters, and people want to know exactly what they are investing in, so be prepared!

The second step is to get your company appraised by a business opportunity appraiser. According to Michael Lustig, author of *Selling Business Opportunities in California,* real estate offices commonly sell for 50 percent of one year's gross commissions. There are obviously mitigating factors such as how old and how well established your company is, your location, your lease, the tenure of your sales staff, your market share, whether you will stay on as sales manager for a time or not, and the real estate market conditions at the time of sale.

You need to be very careful about how you get the word out that you want to sell. If your sales staff hears about it and starts leaving because you were the only reason that they were staying, it could spell trouble, so the obvious first potential buyer is someone in your own organization that you know has the financial capability to make the purchase and has expressed a desire to manage or own his or her own office. Approach these people with the idea

You need to be very careful about how you get the word out that you want to sell.

that you might someday be thinking about selling your office and, if you did, would they be interested in buying it? If they show a desire to buy your company, ask them about their timing. If they are open to doing so "soon," tell them that you'll come up with a fair price and get back to them. *Caution: Be sure to express your need for absolute discretion!*

Wait a few days and get together with them and show them the appraisal. Tell them that they may be free to get their own appraisal if they like, then negotiate your best deal. Be prepared to carry some paper but do not heavily leverage the buyout. I would suggest at least 35 to 40 percent cash down (or a rental property equity in trade), while you carry the rest at 10 percent interest if allowed in your state.

If you want all cash, then the larger companies, such as the NRT (National Realty Trust) in New Jersey, or a large multi-office firm in your local area are your likely buyers. Get your appraisal first, then call their main office and find out who is the contact person for purchases of real estate firms in your area. Write that person a confidential letter expressing your desire to sell your company and ask if someone would be interested in meeting with you to discuss it. If your contact agrees, set the meeting and begin the negotiations. Remember, a cash buyer will not pay as much as a buyer that you finance, but there is both safety in a cash offer and a time value to money that offsets a lower price.

You should be prepared to sign a non-compete agreement when you sell that says you agree to pay the buyer an agreed-upon sum of money if you open a real estate firm within a certain radius of your current office for a certain number of years.

Transitioning Your Branch Office through an Acquisition by Another Company

$\mathcal{A}$s soon as you are notified of a purchase of your company by another firm, or if you hear what you think is a well-founded rumor about your company being acquired, start to discreetly investigate the acquiring company.

> *As soon as you are notified of a purchase of your company by another firm . . . start to discreetly investigate the acquiring company.*

Investigate

Make phone calls to agents and managers that you know at that company and ask them some pointed questions, like:

1. What do you like the best about them?

2. What do you dislike the most?

3. What are the senior management people like?

4. How's their relocation department?

5. What special policies do they have that are different from ours?

Ask a few key people in your office what they know about the company and how they feel about them as a competitor. Be careful about this or you will start a rumor yourself. Once it is common knowledge that you have been acquired, you can then talk intelligently about the strong points of being associated with the new firm.

Communication

Rumors will be flying and gossip will abound. Human nature is such that the "perceived" worst will always be the topic of conversation. Since perception is reality, you will deal with all of that negativity as though it were reality unless you make a concerted effort to communicate openly and regularly with both your sales staff and your administrative staff.

The administrative staff's comfort with the transition cannot be stressed enough. They are usually salaried and they will all be thinking "layoff" or "how vulnerable am I?" They can spread good or bad feelings about being acquired faster than the sales staff, so keep them well informed and be honest with them. Have a staff meeting with all of your administrative staff present and let them know exactly what you know. Ask them to openly express their concerns as well as any positive things that they have to say. If they ask questions about their jobs, new duties, and so on and you don't have the answers, write the questions down and tell them that you will address them with the new senior management and get back to them as soon as possible.

Take the time to think like an agent. What would you be concerned about if you were an agent? Ask your agents in one-on-one conversations if they have any questions or concerns about the transition—believe me, they do! Commission split changes, who pays for what, advertising issues (where, when, who pays?), and desk and/or office space issues are just a few of the recurring questions that you will get. Anticipate them and get answers in advance.

Take the time to think like an agent.

Be around, available, and visible a lot during the first several months of the transition. It takes this long for the culture shock (even a very positive one) to wear off. Keep reminding the sales staff that everything will work out fine and that they should stay focused on their production. Do this over and over again as it does sink in after awhile.

You will be asked over and over, "How do you feel about it?" Be prepared for it in advance. Let everyone know in writing, by voice mail, and by E-mail about any policy differences or changes that are being initiated as soon as it is reasonable to tell them. *Do not* suddenly spring any surprises on them and, whenever possible, give them the reasoning for the change or different way of doing business. That way they feel empowered and informed.

Make several trips a day through the office. Stop, look, and listen. Stop to talk to agents, especially in groups. Ask how they are doing and if you can do anything to help them. Look around. Do you see anything unusual or different going on? Does a group of agents stop talking and busy themselves when you show up? If so, say "Sounds like you guys have some questions that I can answer for you." Listen.

Do you hear anything that just doesn't quite feel right? Check it out and deal with it. Did you hear something positive? Build on it. Ask if anyone else has had a similar experience since the transition. Make a status report about "the move" a regular agenda item at your office meetings. Always "fudge" a little about any dates given to you regarding construction deadlines, and so on. Under-promise and over-deliver.

Attitude

When you encounter or hear about a rabble-rouser, take him or her on immediately and privately. Tell these people that the change is permanent and that they will only do you a great deal of harm and no good by spreading negative feelings and that you need and expect their full support in order to make this work to everyone's advantage. If they continue to be negative, then it is time for a "relocation talk."

> *When you encounter or hear about a rabble-rouser, take him or her on immediately and privately.*

Watch your agents and administrative staff for comments, mannerism changes, or a sudden absence. Any of these signs often indicate stress and are a sure sign that you need a one-on-one talk with them to see what's bothering them. Often, one or more people on your administrative or sales staff will be pleased with the transition and will be vocal about it. Take advantage of this. If you encounter them in a group situation, ask them how they like the new company. There is nothing as credible as a third-party testimonial.

You are on stage at all times. All eyes and ears are on you every minute, especially for the first few weeks. Think carefully about what you are about to say *before* you say it. Be very explicit about statements that you make in support of the new company.

What you say and how you say it will be passed from agent to agent. The more explicit that you are, the less chance that misinterpretation exists. Important issues such as policy differences, who pays for what, commission splits, and so on should be followed up by a written memo in most instances for additional clarity.

Rumors

Rumors will immediately run rampant. One of the first rumors that will take place is that you, as the manager, are either leaving or are being dismissed. You will need to have a "heart-to-heart" with the new ownership about your position early on, if they haven't already initiated it, and find out clearly what their plans for you are. If you are to be retained, be sure to get the word out early and often.

Other rumors that will surface will be about office consolidations, commission split changes, new agent fees that may be added, and layoff of administrative staff (be especially sensitive to this one)! Your staff will clearly be afraid of losing their jobs, so get a clear picture of what the new administration is going to do and work through it with open, honest communication. Your staff, like your agents, will be heavily recruited during this time.

There will be a host of rumors; some of them started by your competition. One of your primary jobs is to address them publicly as soon as you hear about them. It helps to ask your inner circle to let you know about any new rumors as soon as they come up. It also helps very much to just get out in the office and talk with the agents a lot.

Changes

There will inevitably be changes. No company is run exactly like the next one. The agents will be much more accepting of the changes if you take the time to carefully explain them and the reasoning behind them. That way they feel empowered and a part of the process instead of just subject to it.

We went through an immense remodeling of my 16,000 square foot office building after the acquisition. This involved painting, carpeting, and moving walls, and dealing with computer issues, noise and dust, and moving the agents around the office while we did the remodeling. I made it a point to be very available and to be very positive about the end result. Keeping them focused on the end result helped them to put up with the inconveniences they were enduring. We also had a tremendous difference in the space per agent to deal with. By researching agent earnings at the new company versus the old company, I was able to show everyone that although they would have less space than they used to have, they would also, on average, make more money than they used to because of the new marketing plans and commission splits available.

A key activity is to be very public about any positive changes, try to find something positive about any negative changes, and just deal head on (without apology) with a full explanation of any other changes.

Be especially sensitive to loyal agents that have been with your company for a long time. Most will welcome the change and will be very supportive of you (thank them sincerely and often), although some will be nearly devastated at the demise of the old company name that they have worked for through many years. All you can really do is reinforce the need for

> *Be especially sensitive to loyal agents that have been with your company for a long time.*

the acquisition, talk up the benefits of the new company, and ask what you can do to help them make the transition. Any memorabilia, such as old pictures and so on, can be given to them to make them feel more connected.

Planning

There are two types of planning that must occur, people planning and facilities planning.

People planning is about anticipating the agents' and staffs' fears and addressing them in a timely manner so as to keep everyone productive and less vulnerable to the recruiting efforts of your competitors. You need to think like an agent as well as like a staff person. Ask yourself, "What are they most likely to be afraid of?" Answer the questions and take action sooner rather than later, and their fears will go away or subside to a manageable level.

Facilities planning only comes into play if you are doing any extensive remodeling, like we did. Agents and staff that are moved around, especially several times, tend to start to focus on the inconvenience instead of on making sales, taking listings, or supporting the agents in that venture.

To lessen the impact of the move you need to get a copy of the new floor plan as soon as possible. Make several copies, then think out the stages of the remodel. How can you do it with the least amount of impact on the agents and staff, while staying within your budget?

Each time that people are moved around, make a map of where they are now and where they are being moved. Use some kind of easy-to-read code, such as A to A-1, B to B-1, for each desk and/or person to be moved, with A being the current location and A-1 being the new location. The movers, agents, and staff should all be informed of the code, the timing of the move, and what their respective responsibilities are before, during, and after the move. Agents and staff are responsible to pack up everything in boxes the afternoon prior to the move. The staff is responsible for putting coded tags on each piece of furniture, box, or other item to be moved along with a coded tag on each cubicle or office door where a move is taking place. Overdo memos about the move. You will also need to involve your computer and phone system departments, as appropriate, and see that they have maps in advance as well.

It is important to be around and very visible and helpful on moving day.

Keep the Agents Focused on Production

Change is something that few human beings deal with very well. If you let the agents get into a routine of complaining about the inconveniences of the move, particularly if you have a multi-stage move due to remodeling, they will quickly become unhappy and less productive.

Change is something that few human beings deal with very well.

To counter this, talk about production. Make a voice mail call to each agent that lists and/or sells something (I do this regularly anyway) and congratulate him or her, or, better yet, stop by in person and do it in front of other people. Let the agents know as a group how they are doing each month as compared to the goal that was set. Personally ask each agent one-on-one how he or she is doing with his or her sales, then give a short pep talk or congratulations as appropriate. Never relent on keeping the group focused on production.

To counter this, talk about production.

Recruiting by Other Brokers

This will get wild. Some of my agents are still getting up to five recruiting calls a day. It is relentless and will continue at an accelerated rate for months after the acquisition.

The best way to combat it is to talk openly about it right up front, both in personal conversations and in group meetings. Let your agents and staff know openly how very valuable they are to you. I told my sales staff in a meeting a few days after we were acquired that the only thing that I truly cared about was that we were all allowed to stay together as a group and continue to build the best real estate operation in southern Arizona together. I told them that they would start getting recruiting calls at any time now and that all I needed was a name and an address so that I could call the other broker up for them and personally decline his offer on their behalf. They laughed hysterically, but the message that I really cared about our relationship was very evident.

The second thing to do is to hit back. That is, every time one of your agents comes in with a letter from another broker, or tells you that another broker has really been after him or her, pick out that broker's five or so best agents and really start to go after them. The other broker will get wind of it and will usually get so busy keeping his or her agents away from you that they will stop or slow their efforts with your folks.

Additional Revenue Sources

History

By the early seventies, the Baby Boomers had reached their mid-twenties and began marrying and forming new households. This created an enormous and unprecedented demand for housing. Part of meeting this demand brought about a huge increase in the number of real estate agents that were needed to help them with their purchases and rentals.

As more and more companies opened, a keen competition for qualified, experienced agents emerged. Many of the new companies that emerged had little to offer an experienced agent, so they began to entice agents away from their existing companies with offers of ever-higher commission splits. The agents gleefully accepted and the race was on. A large number of these firms failed and closed their doors several years later when interest rates hit 17 percent and business ground to a crawl from the dizzying heights of the seventies, but the damage had already been done.

Once you give an agent a commission split, you can rarely, if ever, reduce it and retain the agent, so even though the market conditions dictated that a more conservative split be maintained, it was virtually impossible to acquire and/or retain all but the most loyal of agents with a "reasonable" split.

At the same time, more and more sellers began to negotiate their sales commissions downward, creating a two-way squeeze on the "company dollar," that is, the money available to real estate companies to run their businesses and still make a profit after the agents are paid their commissions.

This two-way squeeze has gone on for over twenty-five years, and toward the end of the nineties the situation hit critical mass. That is to say that far too many excellent, well-run real estate companies simply could not pay their operating expenses with the meager amount of net funds available to them after they paid the agents. What were they to do?

According to statistics recently released by the National Association of REALTORS®, over 20 percent of the top 500 real estate companies in the United States have ceased to exist over the last few years.

They either sold out to, or merged with, other companies that were financially more secure, trying to achieve a profitable position again through economy of scale, or simply ceased to exist.

> *. . . Over 20 percent of the top 500 real estate companies in the United States have ceased to exist over the last few years.*

When I moved to Tucson, Arizona, and took the position of branch manager for the flagship office of a firm in southern Arizona, it only took a short time before I knew that it was financially troubled and a candidate for acquisition by a larger firm. That is exactly what took place less than a year later. Fortunately, a well-run company that really paid attention to the bottom line and was profitable acquired us.

The profit margins of even the best-run real estate companies today are razor thin, often running in the 2 to 3 percent of gross revenues range. There are many, many companies today that are still running in the red. So what was to be done about this?

Sources of Revenue: Why would someone even own a real estate company today if profits are so elusive?

The answer lies in ancillary services such as mortgage companies, title insurance companies, and home insurance companies that are owned in whole or in part by the real estate company, as well as affiliations with other related services such as home warranty companies, home inspection companies, termite and pest control companies, furniture rental agencies, pool installation and maintenance companies, and many other companies that derive a great deal of their income from the home buying process.

Implementation

Your company may either choose to buy an existing mortgage, title insurance, or home insurance business; buy a part ownership in one or more of these businesses; or open a new one. The latter is not usually done due to high start-up costs unless there is not already a viable existing one in your area and there is sufficient business in the area, primarily from your company, that will support it. It usually takes very deep pockets to be able to buy a major title insurance or mortgage business, and it can only be accomplished by the largest of real estate holding companies; however, it is well worth exploring in your area to see if the opportunities exist for either a partial or full purchase of one of these companies.

In most states it is much easier to open your own mortgage company and, since all of the business will be conducted within your existing offices, start-up costs, while still expensive, are kept to a minimum.

As with any business acquisition and purchase, you will have to evaluate its financial condition by using professionals to see that the business that you are acquiring is on sound economic ground, as well as do a careful analysis of what percentage of your controlled business (i.e., your agency gets to select the title and or escrow company) you will be able to direct to the newly acquired company and what those numbers will mean to you in increased profits and return on investment.

Although somewhat more expensive, hiring as many of the high-profile, well-known, popular employees away from the other title insurance or mortgage companies will greatly increase the usage by your real estate agents.

There are many state and federal licenses to obtain and regulations to comply with when you undertake this type of venture, so be sure to consult early on with legal and tax counsel that is highly skilled in these types of undertakings.

If your agents are independent contractors and you can't direct where they place their title, escrow, insurance, and other business, you will need to carefully roll out the new company-owned business to them by showing them the benefits of using the new services in place of where they have placed their business in the past.

Real estate agents usually develop very tight alliances with a certain escrow officer or loan officer and are extremely reluctant to change just to accommodate your bottom line. One of the most effective ways to get buy-in to the new profit center is to be honest and straightforward. Explain to your agents that the very high commission splits that they

Real estate agents usually develop very tight alliances with a certain escrow officer or loan officer and are extremely reluctant to change just to accommodate your bottom line.

have been enjoying are in danger of being reduced in order to maintain a profitable position unless other sources of revenue are found. Tell them that the company will receive some or all of the profits of the new venture, will be able to maintain its commission split levels, and will be able to implement new and better programs for the agents that will keep them ahead of the competition. In order for this to be effective, however, you need their support in sending as much business to the new venture as possible. Tell them that you don't expect all of their business, but that half or more is needed to avoid unpleasant adjustments to their commission splits.

You can also start a "Preferred Provider" classification by becoming a "closed" office. That is, no business representatives from other related companies such as title, escrow, home insurance, pool companies, air conditioning companies, and the like get past your reception area except for the companies that are one of your affiliates, or Preferred Providers. They are the only ones that have full access to come to speak at your office meetings and access to the entire office to meet and talk with your agents. They will also have a spot available to them in an appropriate area in your lobby to display brochures.

You will have each of these Preferred Providers pay an annual fee to your company for this exclusivity. You should contact other offices in different areas that have done this to see what they are charging and how are they handling the annual renewals so that you are competitive in the amount of money that you charge them.

RESPA Issues

The Real Estate Settlement Procedures Act of 1974 makes it very clear that it is a violation of federal law for a real estate company, title company, or mortgage company to charge a consumer an additional fee for anything that is already a normal or routine part of a real estate transaction, and that any "fees" charged to them by "ancillary services" companies must be disclosed in writing along with the relationship between the companies.

Many companies are now charging the consumer some type of additional flat rate fee or fees as a revenue enhancement vehicle. These types of flat fees, often called a document review fee or other such type of name, are absolutely illegal and should be totally avoided.

There are many real estate companies around the country that are charging a fixed "Administrative Brokerage Commission." This appears to be perfectly legal as long as it is a commission and not a fee, and is negotiated and disclosed to the consumer before he or she enters into a listing agreement or purchase agreement.

This is probably best done in two ways. First, the amount of the Administrative Brokerage Commission should be disclosed in writing in the Listing Agreement that the seller signs and in the Agency Disclosure Form and Buyer/Broker Employment Agreement that a buyer would sign before entering into a purchase contract.

The second way to disclose the additional commission is done extremely well by a company here in Arizona. It has gathered together every conceivable disclosure that could possibly be used in an Arizona real estate transaction and has grouped them together, including a second disclosure about their "AB" Commission and their title and mortgage affiliations, in a packet that is given up front to each buyer and seller. These are called "We notice our buyers" and "We notice our sellers," respectively. The front page is a summary of what the buyer or seller has received in the packet, and there are two front pages with each packet. The customer or client is asked to sign the top copy and the agent retains it for the company file to show that there was full up front disclosure.

The agent explains to the consumer that the company was going to raise the commission that it charged by 1/2 percent to offset rising operating costs that have been incurred largely due to the creation, printing, implementation, and storage of consumer-demanded disclosure documents, but that after a financial analysis was done it showed that a commission adjustment of $175 (or whatever is appropriate for your company) per client or customer was more appropriate.

You will need to take great care to roll this out well in advance to your agents and with plenty of explanation as to what it is (additional commission) and what it is not (a fee). Be sure to let them know both verbally (at a special meeting) and in writing that if the consumer doesn't pay the additional commission that they will have to pay it.

Take plenty of time with this and rehearse it well so that your implementation of it goes over well with the agents. Meet with several of your key agents a day prior to rolling it out to the entire company or office and get them to understand why you are doing it, how important to the viability of your business it is, and how much you value their leadership in the company or office and how much help they can be to you in supporting you in this.

Herd Realty Corporation
Narrative Business Plan

I plan to open and operate a real estate brokerage office in the Westlake area of Daly City, California, on January 1, 2002.

My research shows me that there are approximately 2,700 annual home sales in the north peninsula, which includes South San Francisco, Daly City, Brisbane, and the southwestern part of San Francisco. This entire area is within a six-mile radius of the Skyline Plaza Shopping Center, where I plan to open my office and which would be my primary marketplace. My analysis indicates that my company will be able to capture 13 percent of those sales in the first year, with 65 percent of those sales coming in the second six months of the year.

There are currently two dominant real estate firms in the area; both have been around for many years and are filled with ineffective agents. They are not actively recruiting agents and are vulnerable to losing market share by an aggressive marketing campaign from another firm. There are also six other smaller firms in the area that account for a combined 42 percent of the market. They, too, are maintaining the status quo with long-time, semi retired agents and are very vulnerable to losing market share to a firm with an aggressive marketing campaign.

The office will initially have thirty-six agents that I will hire at the rate of at least two per month for the first year (see Pro-Forma Operating Statement). As the office gains a reputation for being an excellent state-of-the-art place to work, my recruiting efforts will become more effective; as a result, the last of the thirty-six agents will take approximately four months to obtain.

My operating expenses will exceed the company dollar (gross profit) for the first ten months. A portion of my personal sales commissions will be left in the company business account to offset approximately 22 percent of the operating expenses for the first ten months, after which time the company will be in a net cash flow position.

After two years of operation the company's financial position will be analyzed and compared to the current real estate market to see if either vertical (a larger single office) or horizontal (a new branch office) expansion will take place.

A loan is requested to acquire office space, furniture and equipment leases, initial operating supplies, and a cash reserve to offset monthly financial obligations that will not be sufficiently covered by the company's net operating capital for the first fifteen months.

Herd Realty Corporation
Income and Expense Statement
(Pro-Forma)
January – December 2002

First Year

Co. $ Revenue [1]		Monthly	Annual Total	# Agents
Gross Commission Income	Jan.:	$ -0-	$ -0-	2
	Feb.:	$ 5,400	$ 5,400	4
	Mar.:	$10,800	$16,200	5
	Apr.:	$10,800	$27,000	8
	May:	$16,200	$43,200	9
	Jun.:	$18,900	$62,100	11
	Jul.:	$24,300	$ 86,400	14
	Aug.:	$29,700	$116,100	16
	Sep.:	$32,400	$148,500	17
	Oct.:	$54,000	$202,500	19
	Nov.:	$43,200	$245,700	22
	Dec.:	$45,900	$291,600	25

[1] The above figures represent the company dollar, or that amount of money retained by the company after the sales staff are paid their commissions at an average commission split of 70 percent to the agent and an average sales price of $300,000.

Operating Expenses
January–2002

Payroll	Monthly	Annually
Salaries [2]	$4,200	$50,800
Contract labor	$ 200	
FICA—employees	$ 0	
FICA—salaried agents	$ 0	
Unemployment insurance	$ 0	
Medical insurance	$ 200	
Other benefits	$ 0	
Total Payroll Exp.	$ 0	

Occupancy		
Rent	$ 0	
Utilities	$ 850	
Bldg. repair & maintenance	$ 250	
Insurance & RE taxes	$ 0	
Depreciation	$ 0	
Amortization	$ 0	
Total Occupancy Exp.	$ 0	

Advertising		
Newspaper # 1	$ 250	
Newspaper # 2	$ 0	
Print media	$ 200	
Special project expenses	$ 750	
Signs	$ 400	
Brochures & sales aids	$ 300	
Institutional advertising	$ 250	
Agent marketing reimbursement	$ 0	
Total Advertising Expense	$2,650	

Administrative & Miscellaneous Other		
Sales promotion/public relations	$ 0	
Entertainment	$ 100	
Telephone & answering service	$ 450	
Travel/conventions	$ 0	
Education & training	$ 0	
Taxes—personal property	$ 0	
Auto expense	$ 250	
Interest expense	$ 0	
Equipment leases	$ 0	
Credit reports	$ 0	

[2]This assumes a $2,500 salary or draw for you as the manager and a $1,700 salary for the office administrator.

(continued)

Operating Expenses—*(continued)*
January–2002

Payroll	Monthly	Annually
Administrative & Miscellaneous Other		
Dues & subscriptions	$ 45	
Equipment rent	$ 0	
Equipment repairs & maintenance	$ 200	
Postage	$ 400	
Overnight delivery	$ 0	
Messenger	$ 0	
Legal and accounting	$ 100	
Other professional	$ 0	
Reproduction costs/supplies	$ 300	
Stationery/forms	$ 400	
Other office supplies	$ 0	
E & O insurance	$ 0	
Workman compensation insurance	$ 0	
Contributions/donations	$ 0	
Real estate association fees	$ 0	
Total Administrative & Miscellaneous	$ 0	
Corp. Admin. Expense[3]	$ 0	
Manager's Bonus	$ 0	
Total Expenses	$ 0	

[3]Multi-office companies charge each branch office a percentage of the gross income of that office for their pro-rata share of the overhead of the corporate offices. This is often based on the ratio of the total number of agents in a particular branch divided by the total agents in the company.

First Year Operating Statement

	Monthly Total	Annual Total
January income	$0	
Expenses	$0	
Net profit (loss)	$0	
February income	$0	
Expenses	$0	
Net profit (loss)	$0	
March income	$0	
Expenses	$0	
Net profit (loss)	$0	
April income	$0	
Expenses	$0	
Net profit (loss)	$0	

First Year
Operating Statement—*(continued)*

	Monthly Total	Annual Total
May income	$0	
Expenses	$0	
Net profit (loss)	$0	
June income	$0	
Expenses	$0	
Net profit (loss)	$0	
Total six-months income:	$0	
Total six-months expenses:	$0	
Total six-months profit (loss):	$0	
July income	$0	
Expenses	$0	
Net profit (loss)	$0	
August income	$0	
Expenses	$0	
Net profit (loss)	$0	
September income	$0	
Expenses	$0	
Net profit (loss)	$0	
October income	$0	
Expenses	$0	
Net profit (loss)	$0	
November income	$0	
Expenses	$0	
Net profit (loss)	$0	
December income	$0	
Expenses	$0	
Net profit (loss)	$0	
Total first year income:	$0	
Total first year expenses:	$0	
Total first year profit (loss):	$0	

Sample Agent Five-Year Business Plan

Week 1

1. Attend all training classes.
2. Order business cards, signs, and so on.
3. Get desk assignment from your manager.
4. Have a "studio quality" headshot photo taken.
5. Office tour with manager or administrative assistant (where things are).
6. Meet with your manager to discuss your "sphere of influence" mailings. *Your goal is to build this list to at least 300 people.*
7. Activate license if necessary.
8. Join the local real estate association and the Multiple Listing Service.
9. Read the purchase agreement three times and discuss it with your manager.
10. Do the three case studies and return them to your manager for review.
11. Preview at least fifteen of the company's listings.
12. Purchase all office supplies that you will need.
13. _____
14. _____
15. _____
16. _____

Week 2

1. Attend all training classes.
2. Preview at least fifteen of the company's listings.
3. Meet with your manager to finalize your sphere of influence mailings. If you are going to market to a geographical sphere of influence, start your research as to what subdivision(s) you will specialize in. Remember, turnover is more important than price.
4. Start your computer research and a physical drive by looking at any geographical "farms" that you are considering. Meet afterward and discuss them with your manager.
5. Order a "farm package" from the title company.
6. Read the Listing Contract three times and discuss it with your manager.
7. Start to input your sphere of influence contacts into some sort of database. Use a spiral notebook at this time if you can't afford a computer and some sort of contact-management software.
8. Obtain training on Open House techniques from your manager (if you are not currently scheduled this week in the training classes).
9. Schedule an Open House for the following Sunday, 1:00 to 4:00 P.M. Ask your manager for help getting one if necessary.
10. Write and send at least ten notes with business cards to your sphere of influence.
11. Mail out or drop off a minimum of fifty Open House invitations.
12. _____
13. _____
14. _____
15. _____
16. _____
17. _____
18. _____
19. _____

Week 3

1. Attend all training classes.
2. Preview at least fifteen of the company's listings.
3. On Monday, send thank you notes to clients met at the Open House. Tell them you'll call them Tuesday night.
4. Finish inputting your sphere of influence or farm area contacts into some sort of database.
5. Get your client list and picture to Alpha Graphics or some similar company and have postcards made for a monthly mailing.
6. Call back all clients met at Sunday's Open House on Tuesday night and ask for an appointment to show them property or do a market analysis of their home if they already own one.
7. Meet with your manager to discuss your Open House and to formulate your annual goals. Decide how you want to "keep score": volume sales, total earnings, or total escrows. Make a barometer to put in your appointment book or at your desk.
8. Research properties to show, show property, and write contracts.
9. Do research, present Comparative Market Analyses, and take listings.
10. Meet with your manager and set three-month, six-month, one year, three-year, and five-year goals.
11. Get your personal web page done and attached to the company website.
12. Arrange an Open House for next Sunday.
13. Start to assemble your Listing Presentation Manual.
14. _____
15. _____
16. _____
17. _____
18. _____
19. _____
20. _____

Week 4 and Beyond (this is a weekly checklist of ongoing activities)

1. Attend all training classes until finished. Retake any that you wish.
2. Preview at least fifteen homes a week. *(You must know the inventory)*.
3. Schedule an Open House for Sunday.
4. On Monday, send thank you notes to clients met at your Open House. Tell them you'll call them Tuesday night.
5. On Tuesday night, call back all clients from your Sunday Open House to get showing or listing appointments.
6. Attend office meetings.
7. Research properties to show.
8. Show property.
9. Research homes for CMAs.
10. Do CMAs for potential sellers.
11. Call and see for sale by owners.
12. Call expired listings. Ask to see their home.
13. Take floor time as appropriate. *(Be prepared)*.
14. Call twenty sphere of influence people a week (four per day, average). Ask for referrals.
15. Do escrow work.
16. Schedule an Open House for next Sunday.
17. _____
18. _____
19. _____
20. _____
21. _____
22. _____
23. _____
24. _____
25. _____

Three Months

1. Have at least _____ listings from your sphere of influence group.

2. Have at least _____ for sale by owner listings.

3. Re-list at least one expired listing.

4. You should have completed calling your sphere of influence group at least once.

5. Contact the NATIONAL ASSOCIATION OF REALTORS® (online at: REALTOR.org) or the state/local association of RE-ALTORS® Education Division and get a list of books, tapes, or CDs about some particular type of real estate that you want to learn more about, and buy something.

6. Sell at least _____ buyers a home.

7. By the end of the sixth week you should have completed your Listing Presentation Manual. Keep refining it as you go along. It will change as you change. Ask for letters of recommendation from each client that you close an escrow with and include them in your manual.

8. Meet or exceed your three-month goal of:

   _____

   _____

9. _____

10. _____

11. _____

12. _____

13. _____

14. _____

15. _____

16. _____

17. _____

18. _____

19. _____

Six Months

1. Have at least _____ sphere of influence or farm area listings.
2. Complete your fourth mailing to your sphere of influence group.
3. Have at least _____ for sale by owner listings.
4. Call everyone in your sphere of influence or farm area group at least three times by this point.
5. Start your GRI or CRS classes.
6. Sell at least _____ buyers a home.
7. Have your Listing Presentation Manual refined to its final form, including letters of recommendation. Remember that it's never really done.
8. Take a three-day weekend vacation.
9. Meet or exceed your six-month goal of:

_____

_____

_____

10. _____
11. _____
12. _____
13. _____
14. _____
15. _____
16. _____
17 _____
18. _____
19. _____
20. _____
21. _____
22. _____
23. _____

One Year

1. Have at least ten sphere of influence or farm area mailings done.

2. Call everyone in your sphere of influence or farm area group at least six times by this point.

3. Be at least one third of the way through your GRI or CRS classes.

4. Have at least _____ sphere of influence or farm area listings.

5. Sell at least _____ buyers a home.

6. Have at least _____ for sale by owner listings.

7. Re-list at least _____ expired listings.

8. Invest $ _____ in your continuing education (books, tapes, seminars).

9. Sit down in a quiet place and reflect over the past year. Where do you want to go this next year? What did and did not work for you this year? Set your next year's goals and meet with your manager to go over and refine them. The holidays are a great time to do this. **Remember**—You will start the New Year with your pipeline filled with potential customers and clients, so factor this into your evaluation of where you are going the next year.

10. Buy a new laptop computer and TOP PRODUCER program or other electronic database program.

11. Take a week vacation and *get away.* Spouses need TLC too!

12. Meet or exceed your one-year goal of:

    _____

    _____

    _____

13. _____

14. _____

15. _____

16. _____

17. _____

18. _____

Three Years

1. Mailings should be done every month.
2. Make regularly scheduled calls to all past clients, requesting referrals.
3. Obtain your GRI and/or CRS certification.
4. Start brokers license classes.
5. Have at least _____ sphere of influence or farm area listings.
6. Have at least _____ for sale by owner listings.
7. Re-list at least _____ expired listings.
8. Sell at least _____ buyers a home.
9. Buy or lease a new car.
10. Buy your first piece of rental property. *It's the start of your retirement fund.*
11. Take two weeks off for vacation, plus three three-day weekends.
12. Meet or exceed your three-year goal of:

    _____

    _____

    _____

    _____

13. _____
14. _____
15. _____
16. _____
17. _____
18. _____
19. _____
20. _____

Five Years

1. Obtain your brokers license.
2. Mail every month to sphere of influence and/or farm area and past clients.
3. Call all past clients at least quarterly to check in and ask for referral business.
4. List at least _____ sphere of influence or farm listings.
5. List at least _____ for sale by owners.
6. Re-list at least _____ expired listings.
7. Sell at least _____ buyers a home.
8. Join an Association of REALTORS® committee.
9. Buy your second rental property. (*It's your retirement fund*).
10. Spend $ _____ on seminars, classes, or tapes/books.
11. Obtain your Accredited Buyers Representative (ABR) designation.
12. Start to prepare your next five-year business plan.
13. Meet or exceed your five-year goal of:

_____

_____

_____

_____

_____

14. _____
15. _____
16. _____
17. _____
18. _____
19. _____
20. _____

Additional Readings

The following publications are available from the NATIONAL ASSOCI-ATION OF REALTORS®. For more information, call 1-800-874-6500 or visit www.realtor.org/realtorvip.

2002 NAR Profile of Home Buyers and Sellers 186-45-02-LN

Antitrust Pocket Guide for REALTORS® and REALTOR® ASSOCIATES 126-1093-LN. Minimum order of 5.

Don't Risk It! A Broker's Guide To Risk Management—Second Edition 126-358-LN

English–Spanish Real Estate Glossary 135-06-LN

Expand Your Market Training Kit 126-359-01-LN

Fair Housing Handbook, Second Edition 166-1084-LN

Fair Housing Sales: Shared Neighbors, Equal Opportunities Pocket Guide 166-81-LN. Minimum order of 5.

Fair Housing Video 166-150AT-LN

Fair Housing, Property Disclosure, and Sexual Harassment Pocket Guides 166-81, 126-343, 126-49

Home Buyers and Sellers Guide to Radon 141-19-LN

Independent Contractors in Real Estate, A Guide for Risk Management 126-371-LN

Lead-Based Paint Reference Guide 141-558-LN

On Your Mark—A Trademark Pocket Reference for REALTORS® 126-181-LN. Minimum order of 100.

Real Estate Assistants, A Guide for Risk Management 126-370-LN

Recruiting and Retaining Highly Successful Agents 186-42-LN

Selling Homes in the Melting Pot, Cross-Cultural Marketing in a Changing America Video 135-05-LN

What Everyone Should Know About Equal Opportunity in Housing Brochure—English 166-799-LN

What Everyone Should Know About Equal Opportunity In Housing Brochure — Spanish 166-796-01-LN

Workplace Law and Office Policies, A Guide for Risk Management 126-373-LN

About the Author

Bob Herd enlisted in the Army right after high school. He served with the 9th Infantry in Fairbanks, Alaska, during the early stages of the Vietnam War. It was during that enlistment that he became aware of what a truly good leader was, and it cast his fate.

Bob's First Sergeant was an exceptional man, the kind of individual who commanded respect when he spoke, not through fear (although the man was as tough as rawhide). Instead, the First Sergeant's men listened out of deep respect for the way he carried himself, the way he "walked the walk." He instilled the impression that if you were with him when the bullets started flying, he would get you back safe and sound. He was a natural leader and commanded respect from everyone around him without ever saying a word.

Bob soon found himself commanding a platoon of soldiers at the age of 19. Although most of the men were older than he was, he was very comfortable with the leadership role and, using the same quiet authority that he learned from his First Sergeant, he was readily accepted by the soldiers under his command.

In 1973, after less than two years in real estate, Bob took his first management position as a branch manager of an ailing real estate office and quickly turned it into the most profitable office in the company.

Bob opened his own company in 1974, electing to purchase a major franchise. He attained a 29 percent market share of volume sales in his marketing area within eighteen months after opening. It was the top-producing franchise in the entire county every year that he owned the company for well over a decade, and the top-producing office for that franchise in all of Northern California several times.

After selling his firm, Bob managed branch offices for some of the largest firms in California, each time taking his branch office to the top echelons of the company.

After working as the Western Regional Manager for a large California company for a time, the Sonoran Desert beckoned. Bob and Eileen, his wife of thirty-five years, moved to Arizona where he now works as a branch manager for the largest firm in Southern Arizona.

He plans to work well into his seventies and still has a passion for managing a real estate office. He maintains California and Arizona brokers licenses.

You may reach Bob by telephone at 520-918-2401 or e-mail him at bherd@longrealty.com.

Index

Making REAL ESTATE Your BUSINESS

■ **How to List and Sell Real Estate: Executing New Basics for Higher Profits**
by Danielle Kennedy, Danielle Kennedy Productions
ISBN:0-324-18776-9
2003©

This best-selling real estate book delivers the proven formula for creating a fast-track career and higher profits in real estate. Discover the trade secrets to building lifelong customers and gaining market share from the first-hand experience of one of real estate's most highly regarded professionals. In her dynamic style, this edition now includes "money-making forms" on CD-ROM.

■ **Seven Figure Selling: Proven Secrets to Success from Top Sales Professionals**
by Danielle Kennedy, Danielle Kennedy Productions
ISBN:0-324-18751-3
2003©

Learn the sales strategies that can truly lead to surpassing $1,000,000 sales goals! Danielle pulls candid stories from legendary sales professionals to offer you new insight into the tactical strategies and "out-of-the-box" thinking that set these successful professionals leaps and bounds ahead of the rest.

■ **The 3 P's of Negotiating: Exploring the Dimensions**
by John C. Ritchie, Real Estate Learning Center
ISBN:0-324-13493-2
2001©

This essential resource covers the dimensions that influence how boundaries are established for successful negotiating. It explores how different types of people, processes and positional issues all influence each other and ultimately determine the outcome of negotiations.

■ **Residential Transactions: A Guide to Real Estate—CD-ROM**
by Joseph E. Goeters, Houston Community College
ISBN: 0-324-18868-4

■ **Commercial Transactions: A Guide to Real Estate—CD-ROM**
by Joseph E. Goeters, Houston Community College
ISBN: 0-324-18866-8
2003©

These dynamic multimedia guides portray either the residential or commercial real estate transaction from beginning to end. The interactive functions include full video and audio allowing users to navigate through the transaction gaining a full understanding of what needs to be accomplished when buying or selling property.

Cengage Learning is a proud partner in the NATIONAL ASSOCIATION OF REALTORS® VIP(sm) ALLIANCE Program.

To Order, Call 1-800-354-9706
Visit Us Online @ www.cengage.com/realestate